P. 8

THEATRE

THE NEW ARTS
Edited by Philip N. Youtz

PAINTERS OF THE MODERN MIND
By Mary Cecil Allen

THE MODERN THEATRE IN REVOLT
By John Mason Brown

POTABLE GOLD
By Babette Deutsch

MODERN SCULPTURE
By Joseph Hudnut

MUSIC 1900-1930
By Alfred J. Swan

THE MODERN
THEATRE
IN REVOLT

by

JOHN MASON
BROWN

W·W·NORTON & COMPANY·INC.
NEW YORK

THE LIBRARY
COLBY JUNIOR COLLEGE
NEW LONDON, N. H.

Copyright, 1929

W · W · NORTON & COMPANY, INC.

70 Fifth Avenue, New York

First Edition

PN
1861
B7

2/25/41 Hampshire #1.12

20 416

PRINTED IN THE UNITED STATES OF AMERICA
FOR THE PUBLISHERS BY THE VAN REES PRESS

To
Mary J. Ferguson

*T*HE *chapters that follow are a chronicle of some of the major tendencies and developments which have character-ized the modern theatre and charted its course the world over. Their concern is not dates, nor history, in the sense of something that is past and dead, but ideas—the living, con-tagious antagonistic ideas of the contrary-minded that have contributed in their various ways to making the contempo-rary theatre what it is. They reveal the modern theatre only at its moments of high tide, when new men, new theo-ries, new experiments and new movements have appeared, bringing to it the spirit of protest which is so largely responsible for its magnificent vitality. They form the annals of change, reappraisal and rediscovery that have made of the last fifty years one of the greatest periods of theatrical renascence the world has seen. It is, in short, the theatre of these active, exciting years that this book records, caught at its pivotal moments of ignition.*

The approaches to the theatre herein examined have nothing in common save the deep-throated discontent with the established order that they all reflect. Each of them, in spite of the familiarity which may by now have robbed it of the glamour of novelty, first appeared in its own time as a doctrine of revolt, an ardent attempt at reform, the ultimatum of a new order or a new prophet. The Naturalists broke with the Romantic tradition which had gone before them. The so-called New Movement in the theatre —the visual impetus that Craig, Appia, Reinhardt and the rest inaugurated—appeared as an equally positive rebellion from the traditions the Naturalists had fought to inaugurate. From the general order and many forms of its protest came the next phase of change, when the playwright's theatre of the mind Ibsen had introduced and that theatre of the eye, the designer and the director had fought to establish, combined to produce that theatre of the mind's eye known as Expressionism. And finally, as a special manifestation of the constant rebellions these fifty years have seen, Constructivism rears its naked outlines on the stages of Soviet Russia, discarding both realism and the customary decorative details of the New Movement, and converting the theatre itself into a militant instrument, not for any single camp of artistic revolt, but for social rebellion itself. In general that is the order in which the stress and storm of the modern theatre has shown itself. But only in general, for the annals of any art stubbornly refuse to admit that neat cleavage into "isms" and "ists" which exists only on the pages of the books that record them. In actual practice, they defy these convenient but purely arbitrary separations, because they are so frequently coexistent forms, that consciously or unconsciously borrow freely from each other.

Some of the movements described in these pages are already dead, dead as only victorious causes in art can be. Some of them are the dreams of prophets, the visionary men, the theorists the theatre is so fond of exiling to the side lines. Others are special phases, even fads. But all of them, it is worth remembering, came into being as battle cries to be fought for, responsible for new "ists" and "isms," and the founding of those new schools that each lucky generation lives to see established. They are the work of the revolutionists who are always needed to bring flux and experiment to the arts, to save them from the blight of exhaustion, and keep them in that state of transition which is their one condition of health.

JOHN MASON BROWN

New York City.

CONTENTS

THE material of this book developed from a series of five lectures for *The Reader's Round Table* organized to bring authors and users of books into personal contact. The lectures were given in branches of the New York Public Library under the auspices of The People's Institute in the interests of Adult Education during the winter of 1929.

PHILIP N. YOUTZ, *Editor,*
The People's Institute, New York City

THE MODERN THEATRE
IN REVOLT

The Coming of Naturalism

THE red and gold walls of the old Thèâtre Français trembled with the clamor of discord on the evening of February 25, 1830. Surely there was more than the scent of battle in the air on that first night among first nights, when the *Hernani* of Victor Hugo—the young man of the bulbous forehead the cartoonists were so fond of enlarging, not the old man of the grizzly beard—was to open and the Romantics were to fight their way into the French theatre. Had not the conservatives, the good Classicists, who believed in an Aristotle of their own imagining, and admired the bloodless abstractions of Corneille, Racine and Voltaire, listened at the doors while rehearsals were in progress? And had not the eavesdroppers gladly pounced upon single lines from the play, and parodied them with a cruel wit throughout the length and breadth of Paris? Had not the company at the Comédie, with but one exception, taken up their parts with a manifest lack of enthusiasm? Was not the arcade of the Rue de Rivoli splotched with signs that read "*Vive Victor Hugo*," signs that were written by those eccentric young men who were already the sworn disciples of this equally young messiah? Of course. Every one knew that, and more. Was not this same Victor Hugo to be threatened? No mild threat, to be sure, but one that involved death "if he did not withdraw his filthy play." All of the disciples knew this, then, and the graybeards knew it, too, though perhaps they may not have known that Hugo, declining to employ the paid claque custom prescribed, had distributed some three hundred tickets among his friends, young artists of all kinds—painters, poets, sculptors, and musicians—who crowded into the pit, the proud possessors of little slips of red paper, upon which, in a decisive hand, was written *Hierro* (Spanish for iron), the grim watchword Hugo had given them to remind them that they must "put up an iron front."

The scene of the death struggle between Romanticism and Classicism in France forms one of the most familiar and oft-told tales in the annals of the French stage. It involved celebrities even as it changed history. Gautier was there in his famous rose-colored waistcoat, a disciple of the new order, a disciple among a host of others whom Madame Hugo described as "a troop of wild, extraordinary creatures, with beards and long hair, dressed in every fashion except that of the day—in woolen jerseys and Spanish cloaks, Robespierre waistcoats and Henry III caps—displaying themselves in broad daylight at the doors of the theatre with the clothing of all ages and countries on their backs," ready to applaud and to fight. Ready, in fact, to do even more. Because it must not be supposed that partisan feeling or personal devotion such as this stopped here. It soared to higher altitudes, the altitudes, in fact, that Charlet, the painter, achieved in that most amazing of amazing letters which he wrote to Hugo seeking the honor of protecting him during the first nights of this bitter struggle for Romanticism.

"Four of my Janissaries," it ran, "offer me their strong arms. I send them to prostrate themselves at your feet, begging for four places this evening, if it is not too late. I answer for my men; they are fellows who would gladly cut off their heads for the sake of the wigs. I encourage them in this noble spirit, and do not let them go without my fatherly blessing. They kneel. I stretch out my hands and say: God protect you, young men! The cause is a good one; do your duty! They rise and I add: Now, my children, take good care of Victor Hugo. God is good, but He has so much to do that our friend must in the first instance rely upon us. Go, and do not put him you serve to shame—Yours with life and soul, Charlet."

The irrepressible question all this rhetoric about Janis-

saries and a protecting, though busy, God invites is why—
why this feeling, sweeping through Paris, and why this
fanatical subservience to Hugo. Granting that Romanticism was forcing its way into the theatre, that this first
night of *Hernani* came as the climax to a tempest that had
long been brewing, admitting that Dumas-père had written his *Henri III et Sa Cour,* and that Hugo, too, had
turned to the theatre but found no doors open for his
Cromwell, still the question is a fair one that asks by what
special magic did this Victor Hugo, just turned twenty-
nine, deserve these "Janissaries," and because of what extraordinary principles was the Paris of 1830 so enflamed?

First of all, and most obviously because it was Paris, the
natural home of the movements in art, and hence of arts
that have been kept in constant motion. But more specifi-
cally because this same Victor Hugo had written three years
earlier a short preface to his unacted *Cromwell* which had
become the rallying point of a new school, and the formation of a new school acquires a special significance in Paris.
"There is a mysterious magic about the process," writes
George Brandes in a fine paragraph which catches something of the exultation these young men must have shared
on that memorable first night. "Some one remarkable man,
after a long unconscious or half-conscious struggle, finally
with full consciousness, frees himself from prejudices and
attains to clearness of vision; then, everything being ready,
the lightning of genius illuminates what he beholds. Such
a man gives utterance (as did Hugo in a prose preface of
some score of pages) to some thoughts which have never
been thought or expressed in the same manner before. They
may be only half true, they may be vague, but they have
this remarkable quality that, in spite of more or less indef-
initeness, they affront all traditional prejudices and wound
the vanity of the day where it is most vulnerable, whilst
they ring in the ears of the younger generation like a call,
like a new, audacious watchword. . . . Seldom, however,
in the world's history has the mutual admiration accom-
panying an artistic awakening been carried to such a pitch

as it was by the generation of 1830. It became positive idolatry. All the literary productions of the period show that the youth of the day were intoxicated with the feeling of friendship and brotherhood. Hugo's poems to Lamartine, Louis Boulanger, Sainte-Beuve, and David D'Angers; Gautier's to Hugo, Jehan du Seigneur, and Petrus Borel; De Musset's to Lamartine, Sainte-Beuve, and Nodier; and, very especially, Sainte-Beuve's to all the standard bearers of the school; Madame de Girardin's articles; Balzac's dedications; George Sand's *Lettres d'un Voyageur*—all testify to a sincere, ardent admiration, which entirely precluded the proverbial jealousy of authors."

And why? Because in that epoch-making prose preface of some score of pages Hugo—as spokeman for the school at its moment of insurrection—dared to say "Let us take the hammer to poetic systems. Let us throw down the old plastering that conceals the façade of art. *There are neither rules nor models; or, rather, there are no other rules than the general laws of nature.*"

.　　.　　.　　.　　.　　.　　.

Move forward forty years or so in that same Paris, dispense with those Henry III caps, those Spanish cloaks and Robespierre waistcoats, and come to a generation which fits more amicably into the prosaic uniform of a triumphant bourgeoise. Another iconoclast is thundering his ultimatum in the ears of a listening generation, a prophet who has already grown into a myth, a man who has been scurrilously attacked in the press, scored a triumph in the novel, tried his hand at playwriting, and who awaits, without knowing it, the cruelest persecution of his life, the Dreyfus affair, which is to lift him beyond the limits of his natural timidity and gild him with more than a tinge of the heroic. It is, of course, Zola, the Zola of *L'Assommoir*, the arch-Naturalist, the bitter foe of the Romantics, the author of a naturalist play, *Thérèse Raquin*, and a considerable factor in the successful founding of the *Théâtre Libre*. He, too, is speaking the hot words of prophecy, the words which "affront all traditional prejudices and wound the vanity of the day where it is most vulnerable." He, too, is giving an "audacious watchword" to the Goncourts, Flaubert, Becque, and a host of others, a watchword of such a rich contagion, that it is to push far beyond the limits of an humiliated France and score a decisive victory under the very chin of Bismarck. He, too, was a champion, uttering new doctrines, a prophet—come to reform not only the novel but also the theatre. And his words, which were blessed with such a special alchemy, were these, *"There should no longer be any school, no more formulas, no standards of any sort: there is only life itself, an immense field where each may study and create as he likes."*

.   .   .   .

In other words, within less than fifty years of each other two great French insurrectionists were formulating the doctrines of new schools. Romantic Hugo was breaking with the Classic past, Naturalistic Zola was breaking with Romantic Hugo, and each, at first glance, seems to have turned rebel to the same tune; the *Nature-as-a-Model* motif which is such a favorite pattern for rebellion in the arts. When playwrights—or in fact artists of any kind— swear allegiance to "Nature," the oath may mean much or little. But one thing is certain and that is it will never mean the same thing twice. For "Nature" is as different as the men who see it, the times at which they see it, the eyes, the hearts, the minds, and even the racial characteristics through which it is envisaged. Between the "Nature" Hugo fought for and that which Zola championed was that chasm which divides two radically different points of view and equally different purposes: the cleavage between the grotesque and the commonplace, the picturesque and the factual, the Gothic revival and the scientific spirit, the cloak and swords of yesteryear and the slums of to-day. It was in short, the difference between "Nature" (capitalized, of course) that borrows the enchantment of distance, and human nature observed through the myopic eyes of men and women avid for the detail close at hand.

Hugo was attacking the fatiguing monotony of the "ancients," their fondness of piling "sublime upon sublime," and their stupidity in failing to use the "grotesque," which he held could alone lend contrast to literature. His reasoning took advantage of illustrations that in a moment betray the quality of his realism. In such characteristic phrases as, "The salamander gives relief to the water-sprite; the gnome heightens the charm of the sylph," he battled for his points. And with an epic lack of humor he condemned the classic past because—because it could not have produced *Beauty and the Beast*.

"It seems to us that some one has already said that a drama is a mirror wherein nature is reflected," he wrote with a nice forgetfulness for one who was strongly influenced by Shakespeare, and then came to the kernel of his argument. "But if it is an ordinary mirror, a smooth and polished surface, it will give only a dull image of objects, with no relief—faithful but colorless. . . . The drama, therefore, must be a concentrating mirror, which, instead of weakening, concentrates and condenses the colored rays, which makes of a mere gleam a light, and of a light a flame. Then only is the drama acknowledged by art." He pointed out that local color should not "be on the surface of a drama, but in its substance, in the very heart of the work." And his reason was an artist's reason and an artist's pride in his profession. "It is well that the avenues of art should be obstructed by those brambles from which everybody recoils except those of powerful will. Besides, it is this very study, fostered by an ardent inspiration, which will insure the drama against a vice that kills it—the commonplace."

The grotesque, not the commonplace, the grotesque as an aid to artifice, a device for contrast, not an unpleasant actuality were Hugo's special pleadings. As craftsman, he insisted that the theatre consist of arrangement, and that the drama be inaccessible to all except the wilful and the inspired. As artist he wished to be judged by his selections, and have his chosen *métier* insured against the vice of the commonplace. That, and that alone, constituted his submission to the general laws of "Nature."

Hugo's whole contention was, of course, denied by Zola, denied because Zola as the arch-prophet of Naturalism dared to speak against art and its imperative selections. "I am for no schools," he wrote, "because I am for human truth, which excludes all sects and all systems." And then Zola came to the grounds for fundamental disagreement. "The word *art* displeases me: it contains I do not know what ideas of necessary arrangement, of absolute ideal. To make art, is it not to make something which is outside of man and of nature?" And once more, though in different words, he came back to the laws of Nature, though it should be noted that Zola's "Nature" was in both instances "life"—and the difference is more important than it may at first seem. With "life" as his model, even his ambition, he continued, "I wish that you should make *Life*: I wish that you should be alive, that you should create afresh, outside of all things, according to your own eyes and your own temperament. What I seek first of all in a picture is a man, and not the picture."

Zola was impatient with an art that pretended to "arrange" but that "arranged" only to falsify and "pass outside of man and nature." He surveyed the theatre of the Paris of his day—or rather the theatre before his day—and his impatience became as active as only the discontent of new leaders can be. "The historical drama is in its death-throes," he wrote, " . . . dying a natural death, of its own extravagances and platitudes. If comedy still maintains its place amid the general disintegration of the stage, it is because comedy clings closer to the actual, and is often true. I defy the last of the Romanticists to put upon the stage a heroic drama; at the sight of all the paraphernalia of armor, secret doors, poisoned wines and the rest, the audience would only shrug its shoulders. And melodrama, that bourgeois offspring of the romantic drama, is in the hearts of the people more dead than its predecessor; its false sentiment, its complication of stolen children and discovered documents, its impudent gasconnades have finally rendered it despicable so that any attempt to revive it proves abortive." So much for the conditions of the time as Zola saw them. He then proceeded to pay tribute to the change his predecessors in revolt had wrought, at the same time that he declared the independence of the new order. "The great works of 1830 will always remain advance-guard works, landmarks in a literary epoch, superb efforts which laid low the scaffolding of the classics. But, now that everything is torn down, the swords and capes rendered useless, it is time to base our works on truth."

To achieve this Zola hoped to bring the theatre into contact with the times. In particular he wanted to establish a "closer relation with the great movement toward truth and experimental science which has, since the last century, been on the increase in every manifestation of the human intellect. The movement was started by the new methods of science; then, Naturalism revolutionized criticism and history, in submitting man and his works to a system of precise analysis, taking into account all circumstances, environment, and 'organic cases.' Then in turn, art and letters were carried along with the current." The historical canvases, as he pointed out, gave way to realistic paintings, the novel broadened its scope and took in "all the activities of man" and the stage was at last to be awakened by the new impulse. The stage at last, because the theatre, as the most democratic of the arts, is bound to move more slowly, waiting for its audiences to receive their initiation elsewhere; waiting, in fact, as it almost always has, for the new to become the accepted outside of the playhouses before offering it as the new inside of them.

This Nineteenth Century that mothered both Hugo and Zola was remarkable for many things far more remarkable than they. It was the most complex century history had known, in which for the first time the full welter of the modern world was sensed with all its baffling wonderment. Intricate, even confused beyond simplification, a mighty panorama without apparent beginning or end, its forces and its men moved with kaleidoscopic swiftness across a crowded scene. Reviewed in retrospect—and without depending upon those easy and inviting pegs, those key men and key dates, on which history is so often made to hang its trappings, there was not a single placid, uneventful year throughout its entire length. At least not a single year in which at some corner of the globe new ideas, new inventions, new system of thought or experiments in government were not appearing to disturb the mind and peace of man, to tear down the old structure of human life, or prepare the way for readjustments that would some day be exacted. When Hugo wrote *Hernani* machines were already throbbing in the factories. Eleven years before that memorable first night the steam-driven paddlewheels of the *Savannah* had churned their way across the Atlantic. Steam, too, had already come as a challenge to the stage coach and was sending trains across the landscapes of both continents for brave first "runs." In short, the Industrial and Mechanical Revolutions were well under way. And, side by side with them, the ever-increasing contributions of the scientists were making themselves felt—the result of quiet diligence and painstaking, selfless love. More important than any one can say and defying precise evaluation, these contributions from the laboratories were to touch every department of human living and human thinking, and play a larger, though less showy part, in the drama of mankind than was ever played by the glittering personalities who walk away with the spotlight of history. All these forces were burgeoning in that France, that France of tarnished glory, of a dull kingship and constant changes in the social order, which Hugo and his Janissaries stormed. In that same France, too, such painters as Géricault and Delacroix had been fighting the prelude to the battle of Romanticism with such classicists as David and Ingres for a full decade before *Hernani* opened. But in their dramas the Romantics showed few signs of living in an age subject to other than literary change. Instead they preferred to take refuge in a costumed paradise of their own imagining, a world remote from steam or industrial revolutions and reflecting in no way the early dawning of the scientific spirit.

With Zola and the Naturalists, however, the case was different. Science had made fresh and epochal advances before they appeared. The trans-Atlantic cable was down. The Bessemer and the open-hearth processes had been discovered to aid in the completion of man's conquest of metals, and make the "Machine Age" of our own times possible. The history of the rocks which geology told was challenging the Biblical story of the Creation. Faith and reason were contesting in an open antagonism. Darwin had published his *Origin of the Species* and the *Descent of Man* and all the world engaged in the dispute which they invited, the dispute between the apes and angels, as Disraeli stated it when he announced that as far as he was concerned he was "on the side of the angels." Robert Owen and Karl Marx had spread the doctrine of socialism and challenged the capitalistic order; Schopenhauer had preached the gospel of pessimism. The daguerreotype, which had satisfied the public from the late thirties on, was replaced in 1888 by the Kodak of Eastman, the climax of a long series of camera experiments made in the fifties, sixties and eighties which came as an important adjunct to Naturalism, if not a symbol of its methods. These and a thousand other developments were prodding the mind of man.

Even in so summary and incomplete a catalogue, however, it is not difficult to see what those crowded forty years or so, between the Romantics and Naturalists, were bound to mean in offering to the dramatist a new mankind for dramatic material, a new manner of treating him, and a different purpose in undertaking to treat him at all. It is slight wonder, therefore, that the swords of the Romantics should have been dulled with rust and their cloaks left to the moths, or that Zola should have invited science to invade the playhouses. And even less wonder that the theatre should have been subject to the contagion of the age and attempted to submit "man and his work to a system of precise analysis, taking into account all circumstances, environment, and 'organic cases.'" With that as the new aim, in a time when the whole desire was to face facts rather than escape them, it was equally to be expected that the new ideal of the theatre should be what Zola stated as "the fragment of life," (*lambeau d'existence*) or what Jean Jullien paraphrased as the *tranche de vie*—"the slice of life" ideal which is still a favorite phrase in critical jargon and the dominant ideal of so many contemporary playwrights and theatres.

With the brevity of a creed, "the slice of life" stated the aims and hopes of the Naturalists at the moment when they fought their way into the French theatre. But it did not come without forebears, in fact without a half a century of indirect preparation, which gave the Naturalists a tradition both to expand and to reject. Even when Hugo was depending on the stout arms of Charlet's Janissaries for protection, there had been an amiable precursor named Eugene Scribe, who was to exert a far more profound effect on the future of the theatre than that which resulted from all the noisy but short-lived manifestoes of the Romantics. If he did not introduce believable or subtle characters on to the stage, Scribe had, at least, put recognizable types behind the footlights, and the step was an important one. From his over-facile pen came those "everlasting colonels, rich heiresses whose dowries were the object of continual pursuit . . . artists supported by bankers' wives; . . . Legion of Honor crosses obtained in adultery . . . all-powerful millionaires"; and "shop-girls who led queens by the nose" against which the younger Dumas railed. Scribe's types, in his vacuous farce-comedies and *vaudevilles*, may have been important milestones along the path to realism. But his contributions to realism were trivial when compared to the contributions he made to the science of play-building. He was the father of the "well-made play," "the most extraordinary improviser we have had in our drama," wrote Dumas-fils, "the most expert at ma-

nipulating characters that had no life." Messageless, char-
acterless, devoid of ideas as he was, the structural sense of
this "shadowless Shakespeare" was borrowed the world over
as the much-admired model of what a play should be. It
was on the basis of his blueprints that so much of the Nineteenth Century drama was built, that Sardou reared his
melodramas, that Augier pushed the cause of bourgeois
drama to new levels of reality and that Dumas-fils inaugurated the problem play with its inevitable *raisonneur*. And
it was the problem play, built more or less according to
Scribe's specifications, which, by espousing the cause of
moral correction, was to salve the conscience of the younger
Dumas by allowing him to feel that he had performed
both his "part as a poet" and "his duty as a man."

It was, of course, the contributions these playwrights
had made to realism which the Naturalists wished to advance. And with an equal obviousness, it was the sense of
theatre they had inherited from Scribe—the water-tight
structure of the "well-made play" with its infinite unreality and tawdry artifice—which the Naturalists insisted
upon discarding. They wanted more than simple types,
more, too, than *raisonneurs*, who while they were not types
of the old kind were still points of view rather than people.
They wanted life and truth, as they understood them
towards the end of this century in which the scientific
spirit had steadily been gathering momentum; plays that
were true to life instead of the theatre. They wanted what
Ibsen had shown them that the theatre might be. Not the
earlier Ibsen of the poetic dramas to be sure, but the Ibsen
of *A Doll's House, Ghosts, An Enemy of the People, The
Wild Duck* and *Rosmersholm,* all of which were written
before the Free Theatre idea spread over Europe; the Ibsen
whom Björnson advised as early as 1868 to try "photog-
raphy by comedy"; the Ibsen who, though he employed
the form of the "well-made play" was able to put it to a
different and exciting use. In short, the Ibsen who could
present problems at the same time that he was unveiling
characters of infinite subtlety and bringing the tremendous

drive of his intellect to a theatre that stood in sad need of it. And they wanted more.

But before the dreams of preface-writers or literary insurrectionists could be realized in the theatres of Paris—and Berlin and London, too—before "the slice of life" could be cut to the taste of the audiences of the day a man of the theatre had to be found, and the theatres themselves prepared for the change. The deadwood of the outmoded traditions had to be cut away. Actors of a new kind had to be developed, settings of a different nature employed. But above all, it was necessary for a director to emerge who could dispense with the old conventions and establish new ones, fitted to the new ideals. Then, and then alone, could a phrase of theory become, in truth, a "slice of life."

CHAPTER TWO

Free Theatres and New Playwrights

SURELY the Naturalists themselves could not have invented a more appropriate legend for the founding of their theatre than the one which fate had in store for them. For the man who was destined to realize their dreams was none other than an obscure clerk in the Paris Gas Company who happened to amuse himself in his spare moments with amateur theatricals. He "had not," at that time, "the slightest idea of becoming a professional actor or director" and would, in his words, have "laughed heartily if any one had predicted then that we were going to revolutionize dramatic art." This man, who was to emerge from the "little world of clerkdom," be transformed "into a sort of meteorite" and "become the leader of forces I did not even dream of" was, of course, André Antoine. When history discovered him, fourteen years after Zola had published *Thérèse Raquin* and five years after Becque had written *Les Corbeaux,* he was adding a few sous to the meager salary of one hundred and fifty francs that the Gas Company monthly paid him by serving in the upper gallery of the Odéon as an "auxiliary to the chiefs of the *claque.*"

Though he may have had no thought of becoming a professional actor or director in 1887, when his little group of amateurs from the Cercle Gaulois was to win the attention of Paris, it should be pointed out that Antoine had entertained the idea before. As early as 1875 he had for the first time rented his manual strength to the Comédie Française and become a member of its official *claque.* Once he had had the happy privilege of leading the applause at that famous house, even as the great Auguste had led it at the Opéra. But far more important, in the eyes of what the

future was to demand of him, was the fact that as a
claqueur he had the chance of learning "the great tradition" of the Comédie before he undertook to break with
it. As *claqueur* and shortly afterwards as a supernumerary
—for he soon tired of merely directing the applause—he
had the invaluable opportunity of watching night after
night the greatest actors of the time and determining at
close range what was false and glorious in their methods.
"For a number of years," he has himself confessed, "I
took part in the whole repertory, eyes wide-open, ears
cocked for everything that happened . . . and I stuck as
close to the actors as their shadows." In brief, he was doing
what all revolutionists should do, and too few ever do,
and that is of course mastering the old rules before attempting to make new ones. In fact, his approach to the
theatre was so faithful to the existing conventions that it
is difficult to discern in it either a gleam of discontent or a
premonition of revolt. At first glance he seems merely a
conformist and an unsuccessful one at that. He studied
diction at the Gymnase de la Parole and there began his
career as a director with plays written in that very tradition he was later to abandon. He even had his hopeful hour
at the Conservatoire, where he suffered the humiliation of
being rejected because his recitation was immediately recog-
nized by the judges as only a servile copy of Got's reading
of the same speech. Though it was natural enough for
Antoine to have imitated Got, since he had heard him
read the speech some sixty times, this incident at the Conservatoire can hardly be named as a promising beginning
for an important insurrectionist. Five years of military
service followed, which gave him a blunt, plainspoken
authority, and then, in 1883, those uneventful years at
the Gas Company.

That is the record of the man before he was hurled,
without ever quite understanding why, "into the midst of
Parisian theatrical life." And an undistinguished, commonplace record it makes, of average hopes not even realized
with average success. Ten years of drifting, trying to win

a foothold in the old theatre, rejection, military service and the gas company! Ten years without any of that amazing direction or that genius for notoriety which lent such glamor to the Romantics. Here is no general's son who has already won success as a poet, only a clerk who has failed. Here are no Janissaries, no plots against his life, no Robespierre waistcoats and Henry III caps, only an everyday young man, who, though he possesses the courage of his convictions, cannot win the limelight by having the courage of his eccentricities, because he has no eccentricities.

He appears upon the scene with none of those definite, prearranged programs which invite alignments and are designed to win adherents or enemies *before* he invades the theatre. In fact he stumbles upon the men, and even the idea with which he is to "affront all traditional prejudices and wound the vanity of the day where it is most vulnerable." But though he enters, without the benefit of discord, without stinging ultimatums, or protests which fill Paris with dissension, even without apparent foresight or planning, the story of his revolt is no less dramatic than that of the Romantics and *Hernani*. It is in fact, one of the most moving stories of courage, devotion and growth the theatre has to tell.

Surveying the situation in Paris at the time of his emergence, Antoine felt, as he long afterwards wrote, that "The preceding generation was exhausted but still staunchly upheld its comradeship, and in front of it was a whole generation, disarmed and fretting under restraint. . . . The battle was already won in the literary field by the Naturalists, in painting by the Impressionists, and in music by the Wagnerians. It was about to shift its center of operations" —in its usual tardy manner—"to the theatre." In 1887 however, Antoine did not suspect what was about to happen nor the part he was to play in the change. As a member of the Cercle Gaulois who was "wrapped up in the progress of the Club" he looked with intelligent jealousy upon the doings of the Cercle Pigalle, a rival amateur group. He wanted to have his club do something which would outdistance the Cercle Pigalle. He knew that each year his richer rivals mounted a revue and that the great Sarcey, the dramatic critic all Parisian theatres courted, "did not disdain to attend these affairs and to comment upon them in his *Temps* supplement." But Antoine's plan, formulated at a time when Perrin, the director of the Comédie is reported to have said, "I need no new authors: Dumas one year, Sardou another, and Augier the next" was far more important than he guessed. It had nothing to do with schools. It simply contended with a nice logic that "if it amused us to play at acting, there must be other young people amusing themselves at playwriting. The only necessary thing was to find them. My project was adopted and each member started on a hunt." And that was the way in which Antoine, who is so constantly tagged as a Naturalist, and only as a Naturalist, undertook his work, and that, it should be added, was the policy he pursued even in his later years.

The first play to be unearthed was by Arthur Byl, "a one-act play without much structure and of rather naïve violence; but, after all, it was something unproduced." Byl brought to Antoine and his friends, Jules Vidal, "a big gun of this time, who had already published a volume and was a familiar of the Goncourt Garret at Auteuil." In other words, the simple idea of this little gas clerk was already assailing the seats of the mighty, carrying with it a persuasion that was irresistible. It gathered momentum like a snow-ball. Vidal introduced Antoine to Paul Alexis, and the chain letter was spreading, even coming near to "the master" himself, because Alexis was a friend of Zola's, and Alexis "let us have an unpublished act (*Mademoiselle Pomme*) discovered in Duranty's papers." To Antoine the program seemed complete, composed as it was of Vidal's *La Cocarde,* Byl's *Un Préfet* and the *Mademoiselle Pomme* of Edmond Duranty and Paul Alexis. Had it ended there and stayed within Antoine's hopes, the history of the venture might have been different. "But," continues Antoine, "I was absolutely stunned the day Alexis announced that having spoken of our affair to Leon Hennique, another of the Medan group, whose one-act play based on a tale of Emile Zola's had just been refused by the Odéon, Hennique had said that he would be disposed to confide it to us." The manager's eye, with its special sense of values, awoke in Antoine, the gas clerk amateur. "In a flash I realized that Zola's name on our program would win us Sarcey's attention. Hennique sent me the manuscript of *Jacques Damour* and we set to work." And there, in Antoine's own phrases, is the account of the origin of that famous first bill which was played on May 30, 1887—a matter of the rivalry of amateurs and those happy coincidences that shape events.

The course was not an easy one, however, even then with Zola's name attached to the program. Other members of his own club, conservatives who wanted to maintain the old traditions, revive such "banalties" as Scribe's *La Chanoinesse* and keep respectably aloof from sensationalism, feared Antoine's innovation and the notoriety invited by Zola's play. As conservatives they promptly forbade him to use the club's name, though also as conservatives they agreed to accept any rent he might pay them for the use of their hall at 37, Passage de l'Elysée-des-Beaux-Arts. Forced to find a name for his protestant group Antoine and Byl first thought of "The Theatre in Liberty," which was taken from Victor Hugo. But both of them decided with much wisdom that it smacked too much of Romanticism, and Byl, stirring his *pernod,* as they thrashed the matter out at the Café Delta, exclaimed *"Le Théâtre Libre."* Thus armed with a name, and financed by his own one hundred fifty francs from the Gas Company and the few additional sous he earned as a *claqueur* at the Odéon, Antoine undertook the venture singlehanded and assumed all of its costs.

The record is worth pursuing for its own sake as well as in the light of what it meant for the future. "I was in the greatest perplexity," writes Antoine, "to find furniture and accessories which I could not possibly hire. My mother, to whom I spoke, allowed me to take her dining room furniture, her tables and her chairs, for the rear of the butcher shop in *Jacques Damour,* and at five o'clock, when the office was closed—I did not want to ask for any leave, as the publicity in the papers had already drawn down on me the attention of the severe sub-head of our department —I hired a push-cart and hauled our furniture myself the length of the Boulevard Rochechouart from the rue Delta to the Elysée-des-Beaux-Arts." In the scant free time his clerkdom, acting, and directing left him Antoine visited the papers, hoping to gain a few notices for his "affair." But at one of the final rehearsals fortune smiled upon him for Zola, "the Master," appeared to see his *Jacques Damour* and encouraged the embarrassed, hopeful Antoine. "It's very good," he said, as Antoine floundered "under his searching gaze," "it's very fine, hey! Hennique, isn't it true that it's very good? We'll come back to-morrow." And back he came to the last rehearsal, bringing Duret, Céard, Chincholle of the *Figaro* and "above all" Alphonse Daudet. Bringing to Antoine, too, the interest of Paris in a theatre where Zola's dreams of naturalism were at last to be realized on the stage.

Up those same narrow stairs came Jules Lemaître the next night and history too. Lemaître, without suspecting just what this little known theatre was housing, described the scene. "The hall is very small and rather naïvely decorated; it resembles the concert hall of a county-seat. One might stretch out one's hands to the actors over the footlights and put one's legs on the prompter's box. The stage is so narrow that only the most elementary scenery can be used on it, and it is so near us that scenic illusion is impossible. If there is an illusion, it is because we ourselves create it, just as, in Shakespeare's time the audience saw what a sign commanded it to see, and in Molière's day, the action of a play was in no way disturbed by the goings and comings of the candle snuffer."

One other glimpse of Antoine the man is decidedly worth remembering. It paints a final picture of what went on behind the scenes of the Théâtre Libre, before taking into account what the theatre was to contribute to the playwrights of Europe. It comes when the first bill is over, when a second bill has scored a far more decisive victory than was won by its predecessor, and the question of the next program is in the air. Antoine, as shrewd here as he was in sensing the value of Zola's name to his enterprise, is now setting about the task of getting subscribers. He has decided that printed circulars are not enough. Accordingly he sets to work to write personal letters to all of his hoped-for subscribers. But Antoine tells the story more simply and effectively than it could possibly be retold. "All my nights were taken up with the letter writing, and however much I was accustomed to hard work, it was an enormous labor, as each letter was four pages long and there had to be thirteen hundred of them. As it was impossible to meet the expense of the stamps for such a quantity, I carried the letters by hand, once they were done, delivering them at night. . . . At last I had finished delivering the thirteen hundred copies of our program. I begun these rounds towards six in the evening, and kept at it until five or six in the morning. As I had to be at the office at nine, I slept mostly on my feet. The last letter delivered was the one to Clemenceau, in the Avenue Montaigne; and I was so dizzy with sleep that it took me a good five minutes in the rosy dawn to find the house letter-box under the ivy of the little wrought-iron gate."

.   .   .   .

It was from a background of such fortitude, even of such chance, that the Théâtre Libre emerged, the first of the Free Theatres which the end of the Nineteenth and the dawning of the Twentieth Centuries were to see. The parent theatre in Paris was never a financial success. From its founding, however, came an idea which quickly spread over Europe, an idea which was to unleash the talents of a new generation of playwrights and indirectly inspire a major theatrical renascence. Antoine's victories over the deep-rooted prejudices of theatrical Paris and his ability to attract new dramatists to his theatre were all that was needed to give a fresh and vital impetus to a European theatre which was everywhere stagnant in its submission to an exhausted tradition. The protest he had stumbled upon became in other countries a matter of definite policy. And rebellion which had long been fermenting, broke out. Had it stood in need of a borrowed ultimatum it could have found one in that stinging exhortation Strindberg uttered in the eighties when he said, "Let us have a free theatre where there is room for everything but incompetency, hyprocrisy and stupidity! . . . where we can be shocked by what is horrible, where we can laugh at what is grotesque, where we can see life without shrinking back in terror if what has hitherto lain veiled behind theological or esthetic conceptions is revealed to us."

In the words of Strindberg and the deeds of Antoine the clarion had been sounded. The contagion of Free Theatres swept over Europe and minority playhouses began to dot the map. In 1889 the Freie Bühne, the result of much advance critical pleading by such men as Heinrich and Jules Hart, Michael Conrad and Arno Holz, opened its doors in Berlin at the Lessingtheater, headed by Otto Brahm and a committee of nine that included Maximilian Harden and Gerhart Hauptmann. In 1891 George Moore argued for a Free Theatre in England and by spring J. T. Grein had established the Independent Theatre in Tottenham Road with George Meredith, Thomas Hardy, Arthur Wing Pinero and Henry Arthur Jones on its advisory board.

In both London and Berlin the rebels stormed the barricades of the old order with Ibsen's *Ghosts*. The censor had already frowned on the play in Berlin, but the Freie Bühne, which was to be "free of censorship," boldly chose to give it a second hearing, and circumvented the authorities by means of a subscription audience. In London the tempest *Ghosts* provoked may be taken as a last stand of Victorianism against the modern spirit. It was no picayune struggle, to be sure, but a fierce and bitter battle, in which so doughty a warrior as Clement Scott generaled the conservative forces, and Edmund Gosse, William Archer and Shaw combined to lead the liberals. A fair conception of its controversial heat may be gained on those vitriol-drenched pages of *The Quintessence of Ibsenism*, where Shaw has republished the most thunderous bolts of the Anti-Ibsenites which William Archer once collected "as a nucleus for a Dictionary of Abuse." They were no half-way indictments, these phrases Clement Scott and the other redoubtables hurled against the play. Their scope is as remarkable as their gusto and their imagery. They range from "an open drain," "a loathsome sore unbandaged," "a dirty act done publicly," "crapulous stuff" and "a lazar-house with all its doors and windows open" to "merely dull dirt drawn out," "lugubrious diagnosis of sordid impropriety," "maunderings of nookshotten Norwegians," "garbage and offal," and "as foul and filthy a concoction as has ever been allowed to disgrace the boards of an English theatre."

But for all their range, these untempered invectives have far more to say about the mind of England in the nineties than they have points to make against Ibsen. They, as much as anything else, indicate what any sincere, uncompromising playwright of the day was forced to combat, and aid in clarifying the kind of work it was necessary for the minority theatres to perform, particularly in England. Nor did the real services of these "free theatres" lie in the importations which initiated their audiences into what was being done abroad and hence outraged their insularity. Instead they were centered in those native playwrights they cradled and the new talents they encouraged. Because of the Freie Bühne Hauptmann started his work for the German stage, and with his *Before Sunrise* gave Berlin an opening of an excitement and significance in many ways comparable to the *bataille d'Hernani*. In its second season, when a first year that included *Ghosts*, *Thérèse Raquin* and George Moore's *The Strike at Arling-*

ford was over, the Independent Theatre had the honor of
introducing George Bernard Shaw to the English stage
with *Widowers' Houses*. After a sterile century of Bulwer-
Lyttons, Charles Reades, Sheridan Knowleses, Dion Bouci-
caults and Tom Robertsons, the English theatre stood in
sad need of an awakening. Some idea of the paralysis which
had overtaken it can at least be glimpsed in reading what
so distinguished, even so sacrosanct a critic as Matthew
Arnold was led to say about that high-flown and absurd
melodrama called *The Silver King* which Henry Arthur
Jones and Henry Herman had concocted for the delight of
London just nine years before the English première of
Ghosts. "In general throughout the piece the diction and
sentiments are natural, they have sobriety and propriety,
they are literature. It is an excellent and hopeful sign to
find playwrights capable of writing in this style, actors
capable of rendering it, a public capable of enjoying," ran
the gospel according to St. Matthew. And there is ample
reason for finding a text in this gospel of optimism,
founded as it was on a play that is beneath despising and
springing as it did from the dark despair of those barren
years of the early eighties. It is worth noting, too, that it
was set down a full decade before Pinero and Jones as
reformed by Ibsen were to write *The Second Mrs. Tan-
queray* and *Michael and His Lost Angel* and the younger
playwrights were to appear.

The Independent Theatre was short-lived from the standpoint of years, but, like so many theatres of its kind, its
life was long enough to accomplish its purpose. On its
heels came a flood of successors:—the Stage Society, the
Play Actors, the Oncomers, the Drama Society, the Pioneer
Players, and, finally, the formation of repertory companies
in Manchester, Glasgow, Liverpool and Birmingham. In
addition to being given an opportunity of sharing the plays
of Maeterlinck, Ibsen and Hauptmann with the mother
countries, England was suddenly awakened—due to these
adventurous and hospitable theatres—to a new generation
of dramatists, dramatists of note, men like Shaw, Gals-

worthy, Masefield, Granville-Barker, St. John Hankin, Stanley Houghton, Arnold Bennett and the rest. Ireland, too, stirred to the fresh impulse. In 1899 the Irish Literary Theatre was founded, to be followed in 1904 at the rent-free Abbey Theatre, Dublin, which the ever-experimental Miss A. E. F. Horniman provided, by the Irish National Dramatic Society, and Yeats, Lady Gregory, and Synge, writing authoritatively of the Irish folk and folklore, became world-known figures. In Germany the Freie Bühne, after a short two years of purposeful life, had ceased its operations. Meanwhile, such off-shoots as the Deutsche Bühne and the Freie Volksbühne had sprung up, and theatres patterned more or less on the same plan and fired by the same idea had put in their appearance in Munich, Leipzig, Breslau, Hamburg and Vienna.

Even in far distant Moscow, though stemming from a different root, a new theatre, fitted to the needs of the new day, had appeared. Ever since the '30's and in spite of the success of the popular imitators of Kotzebue, known as the "Kotzebuists," an independent tradition of realism had been manifesting itself in Russia. Beginning with such plays as Griboyedov's *Intelligence Comes to Grief* and Gogol's *Revizor* it had been amplified and developed in the dramas of Turgenev and Ostrovski. Now in 1898 it blossomed into a full-blown maturity when, after a soul-searching, principle-hunting conversation that lasted in true Russian fashion for a mere matter of fifteen consecutive hours, Constantin Stanislavsky and Nemirovitch-Dantchenko, the head of an amateur group and an acting school, pooled their resources and founded the Moscow Art Theatre. After patient years of self-discovery and humble dedication to its initial idea, the Moscow Art Theatre has grown into the most perfect flowering of realism the modern theatre has seen. In the plays of Tchekov—and Tchekov was the greatest discovery of the Art Theatre—and even in such dramas as Gorki's *Night's Lodging*, its directors and the members of its amazing company have managed to go beyond the ordinary limits of realism. They

have given it a depth, a beauty and a spiritual and interpretative quality which are conspicuously absent in the
work of most of the early Naturalists or later Realists. Always they have studied documents, and even reality itself,
not, however, as an end, but as a means. Following the example of Stanislavsky they have tracked down "all that
pictures the outer life of men," not because of any preoccupation with its surface detail but because of the way in
which it characterizes "the inner life of their spirit."

At the turn of the century in Russia this new theatre
appeared as a violent malcontent, a defiant challenge to
the conventions of the day. "The founding of our new
Moscow Art and Popular Theatre," says Stanislavsky in
My Life in Art, "was in the nature of a revolution. We
protested against the customary manner of acting, against
theatricality, against pathos, against declamation, against
the bad manner of production, against the habitual scenery, against the star system which spoiled the ensemble,
against the light and farcical repertoire which was being
cultivated on the Russian stage at that time. . . . Like all
revolutionists we broke the old and exaggerated the new.
. . . Those who think that we sought for Naturalism on
the stage are mistaken. We never leaned toward such a
principle. Always, then as now, we sought for inner truth,
for the truth of feeling and experience, but as spiritual
technique was only in its embryonic stage among the
actors of our company, we, because of necessity and help-
lessness, and against our desires, fell now and then into an
outward and coarse naturalism."

Meanwhile the life of the Théâtre Libre continued, fall-
ing into those periods which Antoine has noted as "from
1887 to 1895 against the champions of the theatre at that
time; from 1896 to 1906 at the Théâtre Antoine for the
conquest of the general public, and from 1906 to 1914 at
the Odéon (where Antoine had once been hired as a
claqueur in the balcony)—the final struggle against official
tradition and administrative routine." Meanwhile, too, his
idea was spreading like an epidemic across Europe. New

playwrights were everywhere appearing, of all schools and all nationalities, and thus putting an end to the century-old French domination of the world's theatre. In these same rich years Antoine was ringing up his curtain in parochial Paris on the plays of Björnson, Hauptmann, Heijermans, Strindberg, Tolstoy, Turgenev and Ibsen, even as he was discovering for France—to choose from a long list—such dramatists as Eugene Brieux, Georges Courteline, François de Curel and Georges de Porto-Riche.

In short the theatre of the western world was everywhere shaking off its lethargy. Suddenly it found itself vital and active again, more generally active, in fact, from the standpoint of authorship than at any previous period in its long history. The playwrights who emerged in almost every country were no longer merely playwrights. They were authors who were proudly conscious of being authors, men who had deliberately broken with the fustian of the old theatre, and who had something very definite to say in their own rights. In the main they took the "slice of life" as their ideal, writing realistic, even photographic plays of average people caught in average situations. They forswore the remote world to which the romantics of all periods have had recourse, the imaginative or purely creative flights into a realm of fantasy dominated by prototypes rather than individuals, for the minutely observed details of the close at hand. In their realism they were not content merely to hold the mirror up to nature. They wanted more and, accordingly, tried to do away with anything so indirect as a reflection. Instead they presented—as nearly as they could—the "genuine article." They wrote for a theatre based on the all-important assumption that the curtain was only the "fourth wall" removed, an assumption which was to revolutionize the art of the theatre and dictate most of its conventions. The people revealed by this fourth wall were, of course, presumed to be unaware of the audience out front. They were supposed to be seen as they would be seen if the fourth wall of any living room or bedroom were suddenly removed and an

audience permitted to watch unsuspecting, every-day
mortals going about their every-day business in an every-
day manner. This new theatre gave its greatest pleasure
by allowing the audience to recognize the details of the
plot, characters and settings as something that they knew
and had lived with outside of the playhouses. From recognition came identification, literal and absolute identification of the spectator with the trials of the performers, and the final victory of Naturalism was won, and
the second of the two great mainstays of realism introduced. What followed was no longer a theatre in which
people looked at an actor as he made his "points" and said,
"How well he does this or that," but a theatre in which a
delighted audience gasped, "How true that is. It happened to a friend of mine once."

The Naturalists came and went, the Realists were to
succeed them, the Realists who took for granted almost all
the things for which the Naturalists had had to struggle.
Though Naturalism was to prove historically but a small
eddy in the mighty current of Realism, the realistic traditions of the modern theatre were fathered by it. For in
many ways Naturalism was only Realism when it had to
be fought for, when it was a cause to be defended, a rallying point. The theatre that came crowding in its wake was
still dedicated to the "slice of life" ideal and the theory of
the "fourth wall" removed. Or what has been called by
those who have attacked this continual spying on small
souls in small conflicts, the "Peep Show" theatre of realism.

JUST as the Naturalistic playwrights had had to fight their way into the theatre, so the actors, directors and designers were forced to fight for the changes in acting and stagecraft demanded by their plays. Obviously the actors who were trained in the "representational" method of the Classic or Romantic tradition had to unlearn most of the frankly unreal devices in which their craft abounded, if they were not to be ridiculous in the "representational" theatre of the Naturalists. Accustomed to verse, expected to play not to each other but for themselves, schooled in all the tricks of taking center stage and holding it, disciplined to thunderous tirades and an audience which found its pleasure in recitation rather than reality, they naturally were forced to make a violent readjustment to the new technique of acting required by the new ideal of playwriting. Obviously, too, they could not act *Widowers' Houses, Before Sunrise,* or *Thérèse Requin,* in the same way they might once have played *The Hunchback, The Robbers,* and *Phèdre.* The acting methods demanded by these plays were leagues apart, as drastically divorced from one another in fact as *Ghosts* is from *Hernani,* or the technical approaches of two such contemporary actresses as Pauline Lord and Cecile Sorel. The older methods, however, were the dominant methods when the Naturalists were knocking at the doors of the playhouses throughout the length and breadth of Europe. The conventions, even the state of acting in the eighties, and the changes which had to be made, are revealed in that wistful hope Strindberg—the Strindberg of *Miss Julie* and *The Father*—uttered when he said, "I dare not even dream of beholding the actor's back throughout an important scene, but I wish with all my heart that crucial scenes might not be played in the center of the proscenium like duets meant to bring forth applause."

What was true of acting was no less true of setting and direction. They, too—as integral and indispensable factors in realizing the "slice of life" ideal—had been adapted to fit the new demands. From England and Germany, in particular, came two traditions of production that prepared the way for what was coming. As an earlier, though different manifestation of the realistic tradition, and a significant, even a pivotal, contribution to the idea of ensemble playing and accurate detail, these two traditions, born of this same crowded century, may be taken as sign-posts to change. One thing is certain. They did make the transition easier when it came.

It must not be supposed that the Naturalists, though they were the first to demand a faithful transcription of the every-day upon their stages, were by any means the first to espouse fidelity to facts as an ideal in the theatre. There were others, many others who anticipated them in this. Only, and the distinction is worth noting, these predecessors were faithful not to their own times but to the historical periods they endeavored to recreate. They were archæologists rather than Naturalists, realists about the past rather than the present, men who had little or no sense of the theatre but a vast devotion to history. Especially in England these archæologists were to play a decisive part in the theatrical fate of William Shakespeare and the history of the nineteenth-century stagecraft. They were destined, too, to inaugurate a tradition which paved the way, in theory at least, for the Naturalists who were to come after them.

One of them—which it does not matter—apparently strolled one luckless day into the British Museum as even Britishers occasionally are apt to do. But when he left he carried an idea with him, an idea that was to grow into a great tradition. Perhaps he had been the night before to see a performance of Shakespeare at Drury Lane of Covent Garden. Or perhaps, even as late as 1849, he had dropped into Sadler's Wells to see that performance of *Antony and Cleopatra* which the *Illustrated London News* called *vraisembleable,* because of the indication of Egypt on the backdrops. He may have observed that Mr. Phelps, dressing his Antony with a fair accuracy, was evidently undismayed by the prospect of courting Miss Glyn as Cleopatra, wearing as she did, a costume which might readily have been filched from Victoria's wardrobe at Windsor. Regardless of which theatre he visited the night before, however, it may be taken for granted, especially toward the beginning of the century, that his sense of history was disturbed by the amazing inconsistencies he had seen, characteristic though they were of the carefree and inaccurate English stage of that time. If his interest in the theatre or prints were keen, he may have ruminated on the past and recalled that even the great Garrick, toward the middle of the previous century, had dressed a Danish Hamlet in the fashionable clothes of the Paris of Garrick's day, that this same Garrick had worn the regal robes of the Georges for a Lear of prehistoric England, and thought nothing of stalking through *Macbeth* quite innocent of plaids and kilts. Perhaps, though this is purely guesswork, this stray archæologist was looking at the cases in the Egyptian room, or wandering through the Roman collection. Or he may have been admiring the Elgin marbles the Seventh Earl of Elgin had brought from Greece (at that time many would have been less charitable in their selection of a verb). As he scrutinized the draperies of a caryatid which had lost its occupation, he may have remembered that the British government had thought enough of antiquity to pay £36,-000 for this collection in 1816. But be that as it may—for it really does not matter—the fact remains that an idea, a fine idea came rushing in upon him.

He thought back to the night before. Shakespeare's Cleopatra dressed from Victoria's wardrobe when, in the heart of London, was a museum which might easily be

used as a means of telling actors exactly what they should
and should not do! Was not *Julius Cæsar* set in Rome?
And *Antony and Cleopatra* in . . . ? And? And? He
quickly ran over the titles of the plays. And off he rushed
with no inconsiderable excitement to seek out his favorite
actor-manager. Even if the actor's half of the actor-manager's make-up did not share the archæologist's passion for
the past, the managerial side of his being informed him
that his learned friend had had an inspiration. Here was an
idea which might save the box-office and the box-office
needed saving just then when the horses at Astley's had
proved more popular than the plays of William Shakespeare. Certainly it meant a new attack in advertising. It
was educational, too. And more than that it provided English audiences with a spectacle, and spectacles from the time
of *The Masque of Queens* to *Chu-Chin-Chow* have always
found favor in England.

If it took the actor-manager but a few minutes to realize all the values of the archæologist's proposition, it did
not take him so very much longer to do away with the
venerable tradition of acting Shakespeare in modern dress,
a tradition, by the way, which Shakespeare must have
endorsed and which lasted a good two hundred years after
his death. Over night the actor-manager established for
poor Shakespeare, with his little Latin and less Greek, the
tradition of historically correct productions. His eye for
the period detail—which was in a later day to become an
eye for contemporary detail—was the literal eye of the real-
ist. In fact, by the middle of the century, the tradition had
gained so strong a hold on actors and audiences alike that
it can in many ways be taken as an anticipation of what
the Naturalists were to demand when they fought their
way into the theatre. Only the archæologists battled for a
literal transcription of museums rather than a literal transcription of life.

How far the matter went is betrayed by the determined
historicity of Charles Kean's announcement of a production of *The Winter's Tale*. Shakespeare, Kean explained in

one of the most curious of theatre documents, "has left the incidents of the play alternating between Sicily and Bohemia, without assigning any specific date to the time of action. Chronological contradictions abound through the five acts; inasmuch as reference is made to the Delphic oracle, Christian burial, an Emperor of Russia, and an Italian painter of the sixteenth century. It is evident that when an attempt is made to combine truth with history, conflicting epochs cannot all be illustrated; and I have therefore thought it permissible to select a period which, while it accords with the spirit of the play, may be considered the most interesting, as well as the most instructive . . . an opportunity is thus afforded of reproducing a classical era, and placing before the eyes of the spectator *tableaux vivants* of the private and public life of the ancient Greeks at a time when the arts flourished. . . . To connect the country known as 'Bohemia' with an age so remote would be impossible; I have therefore followed the suggestion of Sir Thomas Hammer by the substitution of Bithynia. . . . The architectural portions of the play have, as on many former occasions, been kindly superintended by George Godwin, Esq., F. R. S. . . . and my thanks are peculiarly due to George Scarf, Esq., Jun., F. S. A. (author of the *Handbook to the Greek and Pompeian Courts of the Crystal Palace*) . . . whose pictorial mind has suggested many important details. The vegetation peculiar to Bithynia is adopted from his private drawings, taken on the spot."

This flora and fauna tradition, enlisting as it did the services of F. R. S.'s and F. S. A.'s and authors of *Handbooks to the Greek and Pompeian Courts of the Crystal Palace* had, of course, less than nothing to do with the theatre. It was on the face of it absurd. But it won ever-increasing adherents even past the turn of the century and trained several generations of English playgoers to expect scenery that was learned, even footnoted. It prided itself first on its accuracy and later, in the days of Irving and Tree, upon its opulence. But it accustomed the eyes of playgoers to truth, literal, detailed, recognizable truth. From the recognition that these picture postcard backdrops of the past kindled in the minds of cultured audiences, to the identification invited by the endless snap-shots of reality of the present-day stage was not as long a step as it may seem. When it was once taken the age of realism was at hand.

Far more important to the stagecraft of Europe as a whole, and especially to the work the Naturalists were to do, were the productions of the Meiningen players. From 1874 to 1890 this troupe that the Herzog George II of Meiningen sponsored proved itself one of the great educational and liberating forces in the continental theatre. During those eventful years it toured up and down the continent, visiting, as Thomas H. Dickinson states in his *Outline of the Contemporary Drama,* "thirty-eight cities, twenty in Germany, two in Holland, five in Russia, five in Austria, two in Belgium, and one each in Switzerland, England, Denmark and Sweden. A total of 2591 performances was given in all." Its repertory generally consisted of romantic dramas and excelled in Shakespeare, although in later years it included plays by such "moderns" as Ibsen, Tolstoy and Björnson. That the Meiningen players borrowed something from the Kean tradition may be surmised from the fact that Bodenstedt saw Kean's productions in London six years before he became director of the troupe in 1865. But they borrowed more from Wagner's famous theory of *Gesammtkunstwerk,* or synthesis and joint production in the arts of the theatre. In 1849 Wagner had written: "The highest conjoint work of art is the Drama; it can only be at hand in all its possible fullness, when in it each separate branch of art is at hand in its utmost fullness. The true is only conceivable as proceeding from a common urgence of every art towards the most direct appeal to a common public. In this Drama, each separate art can only bare its utmost secret to a common public through a mutual parleying with other arts; for the purpose of each separate branch of art can only be at-

THE LIBRARY
COLBY JUNIOR COLLEGE   20416
NEW LONDON, N. H.

tained by the reciprocal agreement and coöperation of all the branches of their common message." In many respects the Meiningen company became a first embodiment of Wagner's theory of synthesis. After the turn of the century and especially after the so-called New Movement in the theatre this theory of synthesis was to become the axiomatic ideal of modern productions.

The Meiningen stood for three principles which were at that time revolutionary. In the first place they attached a legitimate importance to the contribution of the director. They did not regard him as a mere stage-manager. Nor were they willing to place their confidence in actor-managers who were free, and apt, to cut the text or arrange the groupings so as to place the final emphasis upon themselves and their own importance. The Duke of Meiningen and his company, in a day when the older theatre was a happy paradise for exhibitionism, thought more of the total effect—the production—than of the individual. Accordingly they developed an ensemble which was unique, and which offered to European directors everywhere an ideal of how a mob scene should be treated and a production handled so as to get a collective effect. Breaking all conventions of the day they dispensed with the star system, and drilled into their actors a coöperative, self-effacing quality which enabled them to play a leading part one night and, on the next evening, lose themselves contentedly in the mob. In costuming their crowds as well as their principals they did not stop at the mere matter of historicity. They went further, and, while they paid strict attention to authentic detail, they were careful not to let their sense of history obliterate their sense of theatre. In their costumes, as in the training of their actors, they sought for the total effect rather than the individual's pleasure or advantage. To do this they took infinite pains, building up their colors in mob scenes, so that they, too, played a contributive part in their general scheming.

In each of these three matters, the Meiningen players were innovators; and in each they were widely imitated by the leading directors of Europe. Irving, who had been in complete control of the management of the Lyceum but three years, was greatly impressed by them when in 1881 they played *Julius Cæsar*, *Twelfth Night* and *A Winter's Tale* in London. Stanislavsky found both a model and an inspiration in their costuming, and their theories of direction when in 1890 they visited Moscow. "I must confess that the Meiningen Players brought but little that was new into the old stagy methods of acting," he writes in *My Life in Art*. But in other matters he learned much from them. "Under the influence of the Meiningen Players," he says of an early production of *Uriel Acosta*, "we put more hope than necessary on the outward side of the production, especially on the costumes, the historical truthfulness to the epoch of the play, and most of all on the mob scenes, which at that time were a great novelty in the theatre and brought success and created a sensation for the production and the Society." In Kronek, a director who came after Bodenstedt, Stanislavsky found a model. "The restraint and cold-bloodedness of Kronek were to my taste and I wanted to imitate him. With time I also became a despotic stage director. Very soon the majority of Russian stage directors began to imitate me in my despotism as I imitated Kronek. There was a whole generation of despotic stage directors, who, alas, did not have the talents of Kronek or of the Duke of Meiningen. . . . Only with time as I began to understand the wrongness of the principle of the director's despotism, I valued that good which the Meiningen Players brought to us, that is their director's methods for showing the spiritual contents of the drama. For this they deserve great thanks. My gratitude to them is unbounded and will always live in my soul."

To Antoine, the performance by the Meiningen Players he attended in Brussels came as a revolution. His letter, written to Sarcey and published by him in *Le Temps* at a time when Antoine was planning to produce Goncourt's *Patrie en Danger*, paints a valuable picture of the French stage in the eighties. "Since I have been going to the theatre," he wrote, "I have been annoyed with what we do with our supernumeraries. If I except *La Haine*, and the circus in *Theodora*, I have never seen anything which has given me the sensation of multitude. Well, I did get that sensation from the Meininger. They showed us things absolutely new and very instructive. Their crowds are not like ours, composed of elements picked haphazard, working-men hired for a dress rehearsal, badly clothed and unaccustomed to wearing strange and uncomfortable costumes, especially when they are exact. Immobility is almost always required of the crowds on our stage, whereas the supernumeraries of the Meininger must act and mime their characters. Don't understand by that that they force the note and that the attention is distracted from the protagonists. No, the tableau is complete, and in whatever direction you may look, you fix your eyes on a detail in the situation or character. . . . Why should not these new, logical, and not at all costly things eventually replace those unsupportable conventions which everybody endures with us without knowing why? . . . Why shouldn't we appropriate for ourselves the best elements of these interesting innovations? I am going to put a little of what I have seen in Brussels into Goncourt's *Patrie en Danger* and Hennique's *Mort du duc d'Enghien*."

Regardless of the indirect forerunners they may have had in the theatre, the Naturalists everywhere were forced to find their own solutions to the problems raised by the new scripts they championed. In a second letter to Sarcey, written some two years later, when such dramas as *La Parisienne*, *Le Maître* and *Grand'mère* had failed at the Comédie and other reactionary playhouses, Antoine faced this issue squarely. "The fact is," he wrote, "that this new (or renewed) drama required new interpreters. Works of observation (or so-called works of observation) ought not to be played as other plays of the repertory or as fanciful comedies are presented. To get under the skin of these modern characters, one must throw overboard all the old conventions. A realistic play must be played realistically, just as a classic must be declaimed, since the character is, more often than not, nothing but an abstraction, a synthesis without material life. The characters of *La Parisienne* or of *Grand'mere* are people like ourselves, living, not in immense halls of cathedral-like dimensions, but in interiors like ours, at their firesides, under the lamp, around the table, and not at all, as in the old repertory, in front of the prompter's box. They have voices like ours, their language is that of our daily lives, with its elisions, its familiar terms, and not the rhetorical and noble style of our classics."

The demand thus presented was based so firmly on common sense that its logic carried its own persuasion. And logic, needless to say, became an ever more important factor in determining both the conquest of realism and the form it would take. Antoine solved the problems of actors at the Théâtre Libre by working almost exclusively with amateurs, players who were unschooled in the old tradition, fresher, more untrammeled, and physically equipped to play the parts assigned to them. In those first seasons at the Théâtre Libre when, as Antoine has pointed out, his actors "were a constant source of wonder," his company consisted of the head budget clerk in the government office, a dressmaker, a telegraph clerk, a wine dealer, an architect and a clerk who sold walking sticks. Little wonder that these people who had nothing to forget and everything to learn, built up a tradition in acting which was glove-fitted to the new playwrights of the nineties. Little wonder that the principle of fidelity to truth should be pushed to further and further extremes; that Stanislavsky should ask himself why on the stage "all lovers are handsome and curly-haired?"; and let logic answer his own quesion by asking another, "Can it be that young men who are not handsome have no right to love?" Little wonder, too, that character actors should appear—most frequently the off-stage prototypes of their on-stage selves—and that casting to type should become a reasonable commonplace.

As the inroads of logic spread, there was even less wonder in that fact that, when the voice, the movement and the dress of the actor were subdued to an everyday pitch, the settings should also be made subject to consistency. If the archæologists could give verisimilitude to history, the Naturalists could give it to their reproductions of daily life. The step was a natural, even an inevitable one. In that same second letter Antoine wrote to Sarcey about *La Parisienne* he seized upon the essential logic which was to alter the history of scenery everywhere. "And that salon!" he complained. "Did you ever see in the home of a Paris bourgeois a salon like it? Is that the dwelling of a chief clerk? A dwelling without the slightest suggestion of a corner where one may feel as one does in the house of any of us, that there is somewhere a preferred spot for a chat, an armchair where one may loaf, after a day's work is done? I know your objection, the setting is secondary. Yes, perhaps, in the classic play, all right. But why not use a realistic setting, since it can be done with care and moderation and would in no way injure the play? In modern works written in a vein of realism and naturalism, where the theory of environment and the influence of exterior things have become so important, is not the setting the indispensable complement of the work? Should it not assume on the stage the same importance as description in a novel? Is it not a sort of exposition of the subject? We shall certainly never portray absolutely true conditions, since on the stage—no one can deny it—there are a minimum number of conventions that must be observed. But why not make an effort to reduce that minimum?"

Reason questioned and reason answered. And it was to making "an effort to reduce that minimum" that the theatres of the nineties set themselves definitely to work, and to which the majority of modern theatres are applying themselves. Electricity had come, to make the backstage more pliant and illusionary than ever before. The machinist had arrived to invent revolving, wagon and sinking stages, devices by which heavy settings could be built with all the detail, even the solidity of truth, and yet be manageable on the stage. Painted woodwork and draperies disappeared for true mahogany and genuine velvet. Antoine carried off from Heidelberg the furnishings of a student's room to insure veracity in his production of *Old Heidelberg*. Max Reinhardt cut down a forest of birches for his *Midsummer Night's Dream* of 1905. David Belasco, America's most important innovator in the realistic tradition and a perfector of infinite patience, reproduced the whole of a Childs' restaurant in *The Governor's Lady*. The Moscow Art Theatre raised its curtain on settings in which the chairs and sofas lined the front of the stage to further emphasize the convention of "the fourth wall" removed. Woodwings and flies were cast into the discard. Warfare was waged on footlights. Costumes were supplied by fashionable *coutourieres*. For the Naturalists had battled and the Realists had won. By conscious design the actual was everywhere replacing the theatrical, because the theories of "The Fourth Wall" and "The Slice of Life" were victorious. But to many, even while the conflict was raging, the triumph of these ideas spelt a defeat for the theatre. To the malcontents who were next to appear it seemed that the theatre had turned its back on the theatre, just as Strindberg had once hoped the actor would some day turn his on the footlights.

CHAPTER FOUR

The Visual Impetus

THE Naturalists had scarcely won their first theatrical victories when the prophetic voice of Nietzsche was raised against the principles of their school in general. His words of denunciation gave utterance to ideas which were to be echoed many times in the so-called New Movement that was coming. One year after Antoine opened his Théâtre Libre and one year before Otto Brahm was to follow his example in Berlin, Nietzsche turned the fire of his contempt on the "notebook psychology on a large or small scale" that so characterized the average Naturalist. "Such a man," he thundered, in his *Twilight of the Idols*, "is constantly spying on reality, and every evening he bears home a handful of fresh curios. . . . But look at the result!—a mass of daubs, at best a piece of mosaic, in any case something heaped together, restless and garish. . . . From an artistic point of view, nature is no model . . . this lying in the dust before trivial facts is unworthy of the thorough artist. To see *what is* . . . is the function of another order of intellect, the anti-artistic, the matter of fact."

Shortly after Nietzsche had spoken his mind, and even while the throats of the Naturalists were still hoarse with battlecries, a younger generation of malcontents was already preparing an attack upon them. This time, however, it was no literary discontent which spilled over on to the stage. It was a protest born of the theatre and nurtured by men whose concern was not the facts of life but what they unashamedly referred to as the art of the theatre. It was, in brief, the visual impetus that was bourgeoning, inspired and headed by Adolphe Appia and Gordon Craig, and a legion of other artists and virtuoso directors of a new type. It was this same visual impetus which, after the turn of the century, was to invade Europe and America under the proud but naïve title of the New Movement. With its coming the theatre everywhere responded to a stimulation comparable only in importance and vitality to the intellectual impetus Ibsen had once brought to it, or the impulse for reality such ringmasters of Naturalism as Zola and Antoine had fostered.

The protest of this New Movement was double barreled. If it was opposed to the older theatre against which the Naturalists had warred, its opposition to the kind of theatre they had put in its place was even more drastic. For it came as the revolt of artists against both the false esthetics of the older stages and the non-selection of the Naturalists. It was anti-realistic and anti-scientific because it wanted to treat the theatre as a special world apart, subject to its own laws and its own effects, a place for beauty and exaltation, a shrine for spiritual release and bold imagining. It felt no embarrassment before symbols and no shame before imagination. It sought for a heightening in line and color which was faithful to the content, not the fact. Its hope was the unfettering of a new order of interpretative artists, and a new kind of theatre benefiting by a synthesis of talents and endeavors such as the theatre had never known. Its champions gloried in that very word *art* which had been such a source of discomfort to Zola. They desired the "necessary arrangement" and "absolute ideal" against which he had stormed, and were proudly conscious that in making art they were making "something outside of man and nature," something which was true to its medium of expression rather than the life it oppressed and hence truest to the theatre itself. With Shaw's *Louis Dubedat* they believed "in the might of design, the mystery of color," and "the redemption of all things by Beauty everlasting."

The objections to the older theatre's scenery of painted backdrops and woodwings were clear to the young protestants at the turn of the century. To their eyes they were tawdry and unlovely, and possessed neither the virtue of being real nor meaningful. They lacked simplicity and were too frequently the work of hacks, who though they were masters of a fair technical proficiency, had nothing to say and less to contribute on their rights. Furthermore, their perspective painting stubbornly refused to take the actor into consideration, because the nearer his body came to the converging sight lines on the backdrop, the larger he seemed to grow. Then, too, these older settings were cluttered and unreposeful, hindrances rather than aids to the enjoyment of a play. The Naturalists and the designers of the New Movement were not the first to object to the painted scenery of the past. The nineteenth century saw several attempts to do away with it, attempts by such men as Tieck and Immermann, Godwin, and Perfall and Savitts at architectural stages intended for Shakespeare which in many ways anticipated the simplification the New Movement was to introduce.

Long before it came, however, in fact in that same prose preface to *Cromwell* which was both a preamble and a creed to the French Romantics, Victor Hugo had stated an idea of scenery that was to become of steadily increasing significance to the scenic artists of a later day. "The speaking or acting characters are not the only ones who engrave on the minds of the spectators a faithful representation of the facts," wrote Hugo pleading for an entirely different case. "The place where this or that catastrophe took place becomes a terrible and inseparable witness thereof; and the absence of *silent characters* of this sort would make the greatest scenes of history incomplete in the drama." The designers of the twentieth century, who have worked in the experimental forms of the New Movement, certainly have had no concern with history and even less with what Hugo called "exact localization." But they have aimed at making the new scenery a visual participant in the drama, saying to the eyes what the text said to the ear, a reminder of fate, a builder of mood, in brief, a *silent character* of no slight importance. Sensing their settings in this light they have wanted them to be interpretative so that they might be really contributive. For that reason they have objected to the endless non-selective reproductions of reality demanded by Naturalism and Realism, scorning them as unworthy of an artist. They have mocked, too,—as Coleridge pointed out long before them—the blindness of the realists in failing to see that the nearer the theatre came to the true, the further it went from what conveys the illusion of truth on the stage. With Arthur Hopkins, they began to see that "if a Childs' restaurant in all its detail is offered it remains for the audience to recall its memory photograph of a Childs' restaurant and check it up with what is shown on the stage. . . . The result of the whole mental comparison process is to impress upon the auditor that he is in the theatre witnessing a very accurate reproduction, *only remarkable because it is not real*."

Believing, as Hugo had believed, in scenery which was more than an inanimate background, and advancing the idea of settings which were "silent characters" and "terrible and inseparable witnesses" of the "catastrophe," the leaders of the New Movement approached their work in an entirely different manner from that which either the older backdrop painters or the Naturalistic assemblers of reality had employed. The new designer came to the theatre not as a spiritless hack but as an artist entitled to the privileges of interpretation and expecting to be judged as a creator. He was, in short, no longer a scene painter, but a scenic artist, and the difference is enormous. Describing the working method of the new designer, and outlining the ramifications of his task, Gordon Craig named some of the major considerations which differentiate him, and his theatre, from the scene painters who had gone before him. "Remember," wrote Craig, "he does not merely sit down and draw a pretty or historically accurate design with enough doors and windows in picturesque places, but he first of all chooses certain colours which seem to him to be in harmony with the spirit of the place, rejecting other colours as out of tune. He then weaves into a pattern certain objects—an arch, a fountain, a balcony, a bed—using the chosen object as the center of his design. Then he adds to this all the objects which are mentioned in the play, and which are necessary to be seen. To these he adds, one by one, each character which appears in the play and gradually each movement of each character and each costume. He is as likely as not to make several mistakes in his pattern. If so, he must as it were, unpick the design, and rectify the blunder even if he has to go right back to the beginning and start the pattern all over again—or he may even have to begin with a new pattern. At any rate, slowly, harmoniously, must the whole design develop, so that the eye of the beholder will be satisfied. While this pattern for the eye is being devised, the designer is being guided as much by the sound of the verse or prose as by the sense or spirit. And shortly all is prepared and the actual work can be commenced."

When Craig mentions the gradual addition of "each movement of each character and each costume" he touches upon that basic element of stage design which distinguishes it from all the other arts and which must ever be one of the designer's major considerations. For, though the scenic artist is, because of the proscenium arch which frames his setting, subject to the same laws of composition and balance that dictate the composition of a painting, the designer's task is not as simple as the painter's. He cannot concentrate as the painter can on a single grouping, caught for eternity at a single moment and place it against a background arranged so as to fit that single grouping perfectly within the space his frame allows him. His setting must house not only the action of the unfolding drama but the endless minor actions of the players:—the shifting groupings, the crowded scenes, and the single scenes as well. The fabrics, the colors and the lights which simplify the painter's task by being fixed, are, of course, never static in the theatre. Yet somehow the designer must con-

trive to maintain his composition throughout that sequence of movement which lies at the heart of the theatre.

It was, in a way, due to a reconsideration of these very
demands necessitated by movement that what is appropri-
ately identified as the New Movement in the Theatre came
into being. To Adolphe Appia and Gordon Craig, those
prophets and high priests of the changes it was to bring
about, the synthesis between movement and setting was a
matter of vital importance. Of the two men, Appia, a
Swiss who is little known in this country and difficult to
read in German or in French, was the first to appear, and
exerted a strong influence on the continental designers. In
1893 a brochure by Appia, written in French and treating
the problem that the settings which Wagner's operas presented, was printed. He followed this by sketches to illus-
trate his theories. In 1899, *Die Musik und die Inscenierung,*
as translated into German, was published, which contains
the most important statement of his beliefs. Like Craig he
was more than a dreamer or a critic, and was, as his mar-
velous drawings for Wagner's *Ring* amply prove, a designer of the first magnitude. He surveyed the painted
scenery of the nineties and found it wanting, because, as
Kenneth Macgowan has stated it in *The Theatre of To-
morrow,* "the fundamental error that he saw" was "the
conflict of the dead setting and the living actor." His
interest in Wagner and the *Ring* led him to esthetic conclusions which were to prove revolutionary in the theatre.
Doing away with the trembling rocks of wood and canvas
on which the fleshly gods of Wagner had walked so precariously—the Coney Island, scenic railway backgrounds
for sublimity—he sought a synthesis between actor and
setting of which Wagner—radical as he was both in music
and actual stage production—had never dreamed. His
reasoning, as Sam Hume presents it in *Twentieth Century
Stage Decoration* was that "poetry and music develop in
time; painting, sculpture and architecture in space. So,
since the art of the theatre is addressed to our eyes as well
as to our ears, how is it possible to reconcile in a harmonious

unity these two opposing elements of time and space: elements which by themselves unfold on apparently different planes? . . . In order that the music may emanate from the actor, filling the stage ensemble, there must be a material point at which the actor and the stage decoration meet. This point will be the 'practicality'—that is to say, the plastic character of the setting and the groundwork on which the actor moves."

Pursuing his theory further Appia contended, "The two primary conditions for the artistic display of the human body on the stage are these: a light which gives it plastic value, and a plastic arrangement of the setting which gives values to its attitudes and movements. The movement of the human body must have obstacles in order to express itself. All artists know that beauty of movement depends on the variety of points of support offered it by the ground and by natural objects. The movement of the actor can be made artistic only through the appropriate shape and arrangement of the surfaces of the setting," a point, by the way, which is admirably illustrated in Appia's widely imitated design for the rock in *Die Walküre*.

To achieve this Appia banished the painter and turned to the electric light as a savior from false perspective and tawdry brush strokes. "An object or an actor," he wrote, "takes on a plastic quality only through the light that strikes it, and the plasticity can only be of artistic value when the light is artistically handled." In making light the theatre's supreme painter, he solved the question of synthesis, and found a means of achieving the "rhythmic spaces" he sought in a plastic setting, while he advanced a theory of epochal importance to modern stagecraft, a stagecraft incidentally, which is more indebted to Thomas Edison than any one has ever stated or than Mr. Edison could ever have surmised.

Of far more importance to the spreading of the new theories in the English-speaking countries, and as spokesman of the New Movement the world over, has been Gordon Craig. Craig is one of the most many-sided and arrest-

ing geniuses the theatre has known, presenting at almost
every turn the challenge of a paradox. As an irritant and
a stimulant he knows no equal, combining as he does the
attributes of greatness and pettiness. Strange and baffling
mixture that he is of prophet and gossip, redeemer and
scold, Mahomet and hen, his very vagaries and inconsistencies have lent a ceaseless readability to his writings.
Of this, however, there can be no question: He has been
the greatest inspiration to which the New Movement has
responded.

From 1889 to 1896, as the son of Ellen Terry, he acted
with Irving and Terry, learning the rudiments of his craft
as a practical man of the theatre. It was not until 1902
that he had his first exhibitions and not until 1905 that
his theories were first published in connected form. As
producer, teacher, author, editor, antiquarian, seer, and
designer he has brought to the theatre a wealth of talents
equaled only by the theatrical superman of Craig's own
imagining. Working but seldom in the actual theatre, and
even then with but qualified success, this Englishman who
lives in voluntary exile in Italy has, like the best of the
Romantics, had the courage of his eccentricities and the
gift of wounding the traditional "vanity of the day where
it is most vulnerable." In his designs, in the great vertical
spaces of his hauntingly beautiful drawings, with their
lines that "seem to tower miles into the air" his prophetic
gift has reached its highest altitudes. They, too, are prophe-
cies rather than facts, ideals rather than actual settings,
magnificent dreams of what the theatre, as he sees it, might
be. And there is scarcely a designer working in the newer
manner that has not been influenced by them.

In his writings he is no less stimulating. In his magazine,
The Mask, his hopes, his theories, his hates, his idealism,
his egotism, his "purple passages," his scholarship, and his
backfence scoldings are to be found signed by himself or
by an "official spokesman" such as Mr. Coolidge preferred.
They are at times personal beyond propriety, petty beyond
belief, but almost always, and beyond doubt, worthy of

attention. In his books, as well as in *The Mask,* he is endlessly provocative. His style is that of a camp meeting exhortation spoken by the fireside, Biblical and colloquial all at one breath. It is dotted with "I's" and warm with a sense of divine mission. But for all that it has a kind of singing beauty of its own. It is the work of an artist who can write even as he can draw. To try to hold his writings down to consistency is no more fair than it would be to condemn his designs because they are beyond realization. Naturally enough Craig's value as a prophet and an irritant does not lie in his gifts as a logician, which are almost negligible. In the white heat of his epic, truly magnificent discontent, an unproven statement followed by a "therefore" is taken as a point proved, an argument won, and he is ready for the next onslaught. Whether he wins his points or not, however, does not matter, for he always wins that greater victory of prodding his reader to consider them. Irritating as he may be, shrill as he often is, childish as he may make himself seem, he is never dull. And therein lies his great power as a stimulant, because, though working from the sidelines, he has managed to put his stamp, directly or indirectly, on most of the men who have come after him.

It is difficult to find a definite, final creed in Mr. Craig's writings. But throughout them all is an earnest, humble search for the laws of the theatre, and a love for its past and present which is in itself inspiring. "It is because of this," he writes, "because the Laws have not been inscribed, because neither the priests nor the worshipers know the Law, *that all action is useless at present.* The laws must be discovered and recorded. Not what each of us personally takes to be the law, but what it actually is." As a prophet on the mountain he speaks, "And I am here to tell of this, and I claim the Theatre for those born in the Theatre, and we will have it! To-day, or to-morrow, or in a hundred years, but we *will have it!* So you see I do not wish to remove the plays from the Stage from any affectations, but first because I hold the plays are spoiled in the theatre;

secondly, I hold that the plays and the playwrights are
spoiling us, that is to say, are robbing us of our self-reliance
and our vitality." It was seeking for the laws of the theatre,
for a theatre which is true to itself and pure as an art
medium, that made him turn on the actor, and offer the
"Uber-Marionette" in his place, an ideal and tentative
solution of Craig's which has been widely misunderstood
and misquoted. With that special logic he alone com-
mands, Craig advances his argument against the actor.
"Acting is not an art. It is therefore incorrect to speak of
the actor as an artist. For accident is an enemy of the
artist. Art is the exact antithesis of pandemonium and
pandemonium is created by the tumbling together of many
accidents. Art arrives only by design. Therefore in order to
make any work of art it is clear we may work only in those
materials with which we can calculate. Man is not one of
these materials. . . . The actions of the actor's body, the
expressions of his face, the sounds of his voice, all are at
the mercy of the winds of his emotions."

It is the same search for a pure artistic medium in the
theatre which causes him to plead for a "Superman," who
can write, produce, set and costume, light and direct the
play, and invent what machinery or compose what music
that may be needed for it. Looking at the modern theatre
he sees it the result of "seven directors instead of one, and
nine opinions instead of one," and concludes: "Now, then
it is impossible for a work of art ever to be produced
where more than one brain is permitted to direct; and if
works of art are not seen in the Theatre this one reason
is a sufficient one, though there are plenty more."

A passage which in many ways best shows not only
Craig's methods but his standards of work is his famous
description of making a design for *Macbeth*. It more than
anything else indicates the change which has come over
the theatre since the time of Kean's announcement for
The Winter's Tale. In its feeling both against the realistic
and for the selective, it is representative of the whole New
Movement. "First and foremost comes the *scene*," writes

Craig. "It is idle to talk about the distraction of scenery, because the question here is not how to create some distracting scenery, but rather how to create a place which harmonizes with the thoughts of the poet.

"Come now, we take *Macbeth*. We know the play well. In what kind of a place is the play laid? How does it look, first of all to our mind's eye, secondly to our eye?

"I see two things. I see a lofty and steep rock, and I see the moist cloud which envelops the head of this rock. That is to say, a place for fierce and warlike men to inhabit, a place for phantoms to nest in. Now then, you are quick in your question as to what actually to create for the eye. I answer as swiftly—place there a rock! Let it mount up high. Swiftly I tell you, convey the idea of a mist which hugs the head of this rock. Now, have I departed one eighth of an inch from the vision which I saw in my mind's eye?

"But you ask me what form this rock shall take and what colour? What are the lines which are the lofty lines, and which are to be seen in any lofty cliff? Go to them, glance but a moment at them; now quickly set them down on your paper; *the lines and their direction*, never mind the cliff. Don't be afraid to let them go high; they cannot go high enough; and remember that on a sheet of paper which is but two inches square you can make a line which seems to tower miles in the air, and you can do the same thing on your stage, for it is all a matter of proportion and has nothing to do with actuality.

"You ask about the colours? What are the colours that Shakespeare has indicated for us? Do not look first at Nature, but look in the play of the poet. Two: one for the rock, the man; one for the mist, the spirit. Now, quickly take and accept this statement from me. Touch not a single other colour, but only these two colours through your whole progress of designing your scene and your costumes, yet forget not that each colour contains many variations. If you are timid for a moment and mistrust yourself of what I tell, when the scene is finished

you will not see with your eye the effect you have seen
with your mind's eye, when looking at the picture which
Shakespeare has indicated.

"It is this lack of courage, lack of faith in the value
which lies in limitation and proportion which is the un-
doing of all good ideas which are born in the minds of
scene designers. They wish to make twenty statements at
once. They wish to tell us not only of the lofty crag and
the mist which clings to it; they wish to tell you of the
moss of the Highlands and of the particular rain which
descends in the month of August. . . .

"By means of suggestion you may bring to the stage a
sense of all things—the rain, the sun, the wind, the snow,
the hail, the intense heat—but you will never bring them
there by attempting to wrestle and close with Nature, in
order so that you may seize some of her treasure and lay
it before the eyes of the multitude. By means of suggestion
in movement you may translate all the passions and the
thoughts of vast numbers of people, or by means of the
same you can assist your actors to convey the thoughts
and emotions of the particular character he impersonates.
Actuality, accuracy of detail, is useless upon the stage."

.   .   .   .

In the wake of Craig and Appia the visual impetus
spread with a hot contagion over Europe, a movement, not
a school, hence having prophets and high priests but lacking any single leader or any one panacea. The variety of
its manifestations was as great as the number of countries
in which it appeared and the number of talents that were
attracted to it. From Russia such artists as Bakst, Golovin,
Benois and Roerich came to the theatre as painters who
gloried in the huge canvases that backdrops afforded. They
were renovators rather than innovators, continuing the old
practices of the painter but treating them in a new way,
abolishing the false perspective of an unreal realism and
putting in its place the vivid sensuous colors of their racial
palettes. They, too, were interpreters; artists discovered by

the opera and especially the *Ballet Russe*, and the influence of their color was strong and unfettering. It was this same *Ballet Russe*, transferred by Diaghilev to France after the Russian Revolution and the war, which brought the talents of a new generation of artists to the theatre, painters like Marie Laurencin, Picasso and Matisse, who once again reanimated the tradition of stage painting.

Far more in line with the pathfinding of Craig and Appia were the experiments in plastic settings and sculptural and architectural stages which western Europe and America made. A legion of designers appeared—men like Fuchs, Linnebach, Roller, Sievert, Pirchan and Jouvet—with marked, individual talents, working in the new forms, simplifying, interpreting, intensifying, serving the theatre and not the truth and serving in a hundred different ways, making permanent stages, decorative settings, permanent settings, using color, line and composition, and planning backgrounds fitted to movement and aiming to evoke a new response to the play. Architects, too,—men like Littmann, Kaufmann, Poelzig and Strnad—feeling the force of this fresh impulse sought new kinds of theatre buildings, playhouses of all kinds, great and small, circus and intimate, static and revolving, in the hope of establishing a new relationship between audiences and actors. Electricians invented new systems and means of lighting. The Fortuny system which had, with its reflected light, been an important aid to the "artistic" lighting mentioned by Appia was replaced by direct lighting of the Ars System of Schwabe and Hasait. New dimmers, spotlights, borders, balcony strips and sources of control were perfected. The machines the engineers had devised to move heavy settings, were amplified so that not only the whole stage but segments of its surface were capable of independent elevation. And the war on the monotony and limitations of the flat stage floor, which was later to acquire a special form in Revolutionary Russia, was commenced.

In America, too, the New Movement made itself felt, revealing a kind of beauty both the Realists and the older

men had shut out of the theatre. It is but a scant fifteen
years or so since it first reached New York, but in that
time designers of such quality as Joseph Urban, Robert
Edmond Jones, Lee Simonson and Norman-Bel Geddes
have emerged, as much prophets, high priests and chief
practitioners in the scenic renascence America was to see
as Craig and Appia were to Europe. They were the advance-guard and are still the leaders, having given the contemporary American theatre many of its most exciting
and exaltant moments. Already, however, a younger generation has followed them, which includes such hopeful and
accomplished scenic artists as Jo Mielziner, Boris Aronson,
and Donald Oenslager. In Europe and America the new
designers have made their great mistakes. They have hurt
plays and productions by turning them into scene-maker's
holidays, which were as harmful as any of the examples of
willful exhibitionism the older actors ever afforded. But at
their best they have liberated a kind of beauty and granted
an unsuspected meaning to the plays they have set. At
their best, too, they have sensed the subsidiary and yet
evocative responsibilities of their calling, realizing with
Arthur Hopkins that "the stage setting of an artist never
seeks to be a complete thing. It is part of something infinite that trails along the ground, but the part that trails
opens within the beholders vistas—glorious, grotesque,
breathless—vistas that eye has never beheld, and these are
the vistas wherein the artist has found the essence, and if
the artist and the beholder be blessed, the beholder finds
it too."

Meanwhile a director of a new sort had appeared, ready
and anxious to work with the designer. He was the practical man of the theatre who could realize the dreams of
the scenic artist. No longer content to be a servile figure,
secondary to the actor or the playwright, he has seen his
function in a new light. He, too, has claimed the rights of
an interpretative artist and pointed out the needs of his
complete artistic authority. Maintaining that the actor had
no right to treat a play as vehicle, he also contended that

the playwright, as a literary man, was not the person to dominate the theatre. It was, as he saw it, a theatre man, who alone could coördinate and fuse the whole production into a cogent whole. And it was as such a man that the new director emerged. Spurning the idea of "the play's the thing," he offered in its place the truer theatrical truth, "the production's the thing." This new director was an autocrat, a final interpreter, who orchestrated the entire performance, treating the script as a conductor would treat a score under his baton, and making of each production a statement of the play as seen through his temperament. Naturally he was interested in groupings, in movement, in color and arrangement. Like the designer he sought for plays that gave him the freest expression of his individual talents. And, like the designer, because he found the cupboard of the modern realistic drama empty of opportunities, he was forced to turn to the great romantic dramas of the past, and particularly to the plays of Shakespeare.

Of directors of this new caliber and kind there have been many in Europe, but, up to the present, none has so far made himself felt in America. In many ways the most typical is Max Reinhardt, a superman in energy, with a restless, hungry desire for fresh experiment which has kept him in constant revolt not only from the theatre but also from himself. Having no definite, at least no apparent, artistic creed except that which each new production may present, borrowing freely when he stands in need of borrowing, he has been the master showman, the Barnum of the New Movement. An interesting mixture of genius and opportunist, of artist and administrator, his tireless drive has led him through almost the full rounds of the modern theatre. In realism he had his beginning under Otto Brahm. But he soon broke from Brahm and became—as he apparently must in all that he undertakes—a "super"-realist in his own rights. Inspired by Craig (Craig would say more than that) he emerged as the champion of the new ideas. Then the spectacle caught his eye and he aimed at the super-spectacle. He first dedicated himself to the "theatre

of the five thousand" when he tried mob productions at
the Grosses Schauspielhaus in Berlin, and then rushed off
to Vienna to reopen the Redoutensaal, Maria Theresa's
baroque ballroom, as a theatre for the "five hundred." And
now, in his new theatres in Berlin and Vienna, he has
returned, except for his summer spectacles at Salzburg, to
what is known as "neo-realism."

There were many other virtuoso directors, of course.
Typical of these are Jessner in Berlin who is associated
with his exciting but often obvious use of steps as a
physical symbol for the spiritual ascent or descent of a
drama's leading character; and Copeau, who on the architectural stage of the Vieux Colombier in Paris did away
with the designer and provided a background of Eliza-
bethan simplicity. The list is a long one, however, includ-
ing Granville-Barker in London, Kvapil and Hilar in
Prague, Hevesi in Budapest, Harald Andre at the Royal
Opera in Stockholm; Lugné-Poë, Jouvet, Pitoev, and Dul-
lin in Paris; and Stanislavsky, Tairov, Vachtangov and
Meierhold in Russia:—men whose methods of work are as
diversified as those which the designers have employed.
But all of them have this in common. They are men of
the theatre, not scientists or novelists, or poets or actors.
They, too, have felt the impact of the visual impetus, and
have in most cases worked hand in hand with their designers: Reinhardt with Stern, Jessner with Pirchan, Weichert
with Sievert, and Arthur Hopkins with Robert Edmond
Jones. Together they have waged war on facts and actual-
ities, fighting for a theatre of the imagination, aiming at a
theatre of spiritual release rather than of detailed recognition. And their chiefest weapon of conquest has been the
eye of the beholder, awakened from a long rest, granted a
vision that sees beyond the everyday, into that special
world of meaning and suggestion, of rapture and beauty
which lie within the theatre's province to evoke.

CHAPTER FIVE

Playwrights of Protest

THE visual impetus of the New Movement was by no means the only revolt from realism the modern theatre was to see. There were playwrights, too, who soon turned their backs on the "notebook psychology" for which Nietzsche said it stood and shared his contempt for its "constant spying on reality" and its "lying in the dust before trivial facts." They were men who were neither satsified with the habitual forms of realism nor contented with the basic aims which motivated it, men who rebelled against its preordained concern with appearances and hated the technical clichés through which it spoke. They felt that Zola's complaint against arrangement—which inspired the Naturalists—had had but little influence on the realists who came after him, because they had reverted without a struggle to the "well-made play" in a form that was but slightly altered. They fretted, too, under the confinement of the conventional play of three or four acts, lodging their complaints, however, not against arrangement in general but the particular kind of arrangement it necessitated. Unlike Zola's, their criticism sprang from a conviction that the ordinary realistic play was an art form which as a form was lacking in true selection, real truth or opportunities above the humdrum.

These playwrights, who for convenience were later to be labeled "Expressionists," wanted to do more than contemplate the surface of things. They sought for deeper conflicts than those granted by the good old external "situations" of the "well-made plays"—even as treated by the realists. They looked for a freer means of presentation and a wider range of narrative than their restricted formula afforded. They wanted to see not the surface alone, but beneath the surface too. It was Stanislavsky who said "realism ends where the superconscious begins," and the superconscious was the object of their quest. They hoped to enjoy something of that sense of omniscience which is the usual province of the novelist, to exercise his freedom in selecting one character through which to see events, and to write with a point of view which was impossible when "the fourth wall" was removed and a mere "slice of life" revealed. They wanted to look within their characters, treat them subjectively, tap their streams of consciousness if need be, penetrate into their innermost beings, and lay bare their dreams, their inhibitions, and the hidden workings of their minds:—reactions and mental states which could not be included in the external observation of the camera. In short, they sought the eye of the X-ray instead of the camera's.

In pursuing their aims, they did not want to concentrate on one event, but on a series of events—pivotal, revelatory moments which were free of claptrap and innocent of padding, moments which marched bravely into the essence of the event, which determined character or registered growth or retrogression, crucial moments of crisis rather than half hours of preparation. They sought biographies, or at least partial biographies, rather than single instances. Like the designers, they were not afraid of symbols, and, like the designers, they too employed suggestion rather than representation. Frequently they forswore particularized characters tagged with definite names. In their place they chose, as the old morality plays had chosen, a man, a woman, any man, any woman, everyman, everywoman, and set them against the background of their time, types not individuals, freighted with a full charge of symbolism. Occasionally they even dispensed with types, replacing them by groups, sections of the community, choruses caught at moments of revolt, or seen as victims of the machine age which surrounded them. If, however, they pursued individualized characters they did so with an interest which was centered in a series of events rather than a single and arbitrary quandary.

As their concern frequently was not the outer world at all but the inner life of the mind and spirit, they availed themselves of the discoveries and the language of the newer psychologists, and particularly the psychoanalysts and psychiatrists who had appeared since the turn of the century. Just as Darwin and the budding scientific spirit had anticipated in the world of thought a tendency which was to enter the playhouses some twenty years later under the name of Naturalism, so Freud and Jung were the trailbreakers of the Expressionistic playwrights; dramatists, by the way, who first became marked enough in their tendencies to win a label some twenty years after Freud had made his earliest explorations in dreams, hysteria and the subconscious.

In the purely technical matters of playmaking these insurgent dramatists found much to condemn in the customary form of the realistic play that pretended to realism. They felt, with a warrantable conviction, that its regulation acts of a certain fixed and inviolable length were external divisions which had less than nothing to do with the treatment required by the subject at hand. To them these acts of traditional length were the epitome of the anti-realistic because, for one thing, it was necessary to place them in rooms in which all the characters might logically assemble at a logical hour; and, for another, because the length of the act was usually much more than its main situation needed or could stand. Accordingly they objected to the manner in which the "well-made plays" were padded to fill, given sub-plots, minor characters, comic relief and a lesser love interest which were as artificial as they were unimportant and distracting. The Expressionists looked with disfavor upon the patient preparation of such plays. To them this habit of devoting one act to exposition, another one or two acts to realizing the complication, and a final one to extrication was as wasteful as it was false. Usually built around one "big scene" or "situation" these plays had none

of the sweep of life—its pace, its confusion, its mad, un-
faltering onrush—and gave, to their thinking, none of the
kaleidoscopic sequence of events or the true complexities of
character. As the Expressionists saw them they took into
account only what men said, never what they left unsaid,
and were, accordingly, eternally preoccupied with surfaces
and appearances. They included too many characters to let
any one of them be fully revealed or honestly observed.
The very dialogue they employed was a matter of super-
ficial epigrams or trivial small talk, artificially manufac-
tured and polished by stylists, thrust down the throats of
characters rather than springing naturally to their lips.
It was neither self-searching, nor completely unveiling, because it was used to show not the dual nature of the inner
man, but that single aspect of the outer man which the
other characters and the audience were allowed to hear.
It was, moreover, unfitted to the needs of that new center
of conflict these insurgent playwrights had found. For
they were not satisfied with the old sources of action. They,
like their times, had stumbled upon new ones. They did not
want to present mankind grappling with outside forces.
Rather they sought to dramatize his struggle with himself.
And for this the old dialogue was patently inadequate.

   In their search for freedom the Expressionists turned,
consciously or unconsciously, to the models the Elizabethans afforded. Shakespeare and his contemporaries had felt
no need for lengthy acts that outstayed their dramatic
necessity. They had spun their dramas on a stage bare of
details but rich in suggestion, and told them by means of
a quickly unfolding series of scenes caught only at their
moments of fullest need and most vigorous meaning.
Their plays had been active, wasting no time on such in-
directions as "cover scenes" or concealed exposition which
are tricks that modern dramatists have brought to a labo-
rious perfection. Instead they had marched to their points
and their conclusions with a superb freedom. No Unities
had stood in their way, nor had they bowed to any of the
academic niceties which sapped the vitality of the French

Classicists. Their stage was the world and their scripts wer
nomads traveling at will to its furthest corners, jumpin,
from Rome to Alexandria or England to France with n
other consideration in view than an adamant desire fo
dramatic effectiveness. Accordingly in the breathless pac
of a *Dr. Faustus* or an *Antony and Cleopatra*, the Expres
sionists found a form suited to their needs. They did no
borrow it wholesale, however, but put it to a new use. Fo
where the Elizabethans had developed a technique whicl
was hospitable to their vital, sprawling yarns, the Expres
sionists looked for one which would give them psychologi
cal freedom of a similar kind.

Undoubtedly the Expressionists were as much influence
by the motion pictures as they were by the novelists, th
psychoanalysts, or, for that matter, the Elizabethans. Th
camera's eye was a roving eye, able to look at its char
acters only when they were doing something, and the
turn with a prompt impatience to the next event as soon a
the first was over. It was never stationary. More than tha
it was constantly switching to fresh and arresting points o
vantage. Steadily trained as it was, on moments of realize
conflict, it possessed a ubiquity of which even the Eliza
bethans had never dreamed. But ubiquity was not its onl
claim to envy because it was also prepared to change it
focus at will, shifting from "long shots" to "close-ups
with a suppleness which, to say the least, must have of
fered an inviting model to dramatists who had for severa
generations been subjected to the unvarying form of th
three- or four-act play.

Be that as it may, the Expressionist appeared, prepared
as Rosamond Gilder has said, to "let off his gatling gu
of experiences—a volley of scenes in rapid succession, eacl
one complete, climactic, independent, connected only b
the thread of life itself—the life of the human bein
whose individual and typical experience it unfolded." H
was ready and anxious to use both the aside and the solilo
quy, for, having cast the ordinary tenets of realism t
the wind, he sought both of these once despised devices a

the simplest means of reaching the inner processes of his principal characters. As a literary form, the plays he wrote were drama stripped to its most basic essence, just as the settings of the New Movement were scenery stripped to its most basic essence. Certainly, as a dramatic form, this came nearest to the ideals of the directors and designers who, faced with the endless living rooms and kitchens of photographic realism, had been forced to seek opportunities equal to their aims in the romantic drama of the past. In the stream of this Expressionistic protest, the leaders of the New Movement and the modern playwrights, who had been pursuing simultaneous but separate courses, approached the closest union the contemporary theatre has seen. Because in it, the theatre of the mind the playwright had inaugurated joined hands with the theatre of the eye the New Movement had inspired, and the result was that theatre of the mind's eye which was to be known as Expressionism.

Though the playwrights using its technique have won a common title they have but rarely been consolidated into a group or school. In spite of certain similarities in "methods of attack" and, above all, in the common desire for experimentation which has characterized their work the world over, the protest of the Expressionists has been largely individual. Frequently, in fact, the tag of Expressionism has been loosely and incorrectly used as a synonym for any kind of definite experiment in playwriting or any kind of anti-realistic stunt in production. At its best it has resulted not half so much from a studious or self-conscious preoccupation with external modes, as from a spontaneous and internal relationship between form and content. In Europe and America it has been the weapon of men who were discontented with the clichés of everyday playwriting and the salvation of those who have had something to say which could not be said in the traditional way. At its worst it has been the refuge of imitators who have had nothing to say and who have had the bad judgment to turn to a form which demands, above all others, not only something to say, but "beneath it," as Ludwig Lewisohn has pointed out, "a fundamental brain work, thinking as resilient as steel and as clear-cut as agate."

To find a first manifestation of Expressionism is difficult beyond possibility, because Expressionism, like all artistic developments, is so inseparably linked with what preceded it both in and out of the theatre, in the arts and in living, in the sciences and in thought, that there is no single moment, nor any single instance, which marks its birth. In an abstract way and as an origin outside of the playhouses, Nietzsche may be taken as its courier, the Nietzsche of *Thus Spake Zarathustra*, that magnificent soliloquy of protestant self-probing which in its thinking, its questioning, and its prophetic note has so much in common with what the so-called Expressionists were to do later. Inside of the theatre the first foreshadowing may possibly be seen in the symbolism of Ibsen's later plays, in *Little Eyolf*, *When We Dead Awaken* and *The Master Builder*, though Ibsen's own reaction to such a statement raises an interesting conjecture. In any case it was of the speech of Hilda and Solness in *The Master Builder* that Maeterlinck said, "it resembles nothing we have ever heard," blending as it does in "one expression both the inner and the outer dialogue." Strindberg was, however, the first practitioner of the newer aims to cast the unmistakable shadow of his influence over those who were to follow him. It was a different Strindberg from the author of *Miss Julie* and *The Stronger*, a Strindberg who had put Naturalism behind him, and suffered the partial insanity of those dark years recorded in the agonizing, introspective pages of *The Inferno*. It was, oddly enough, as Donald Clive Stuart has indicated in *The Development of Dramatic Art*, a Strindberg who after the "Inferno years" (1896-1899) had awakened, as he himself said, to "find Maeterlinck again, and then he seemed like a new land and a new era." It was Maeterlinck, the mystic and the symbolist, who captured his imagination, the Maeterlinck who had stated his famous

theory of inactive drama, his conviction that a motionless
old man, who gives an "unconscious ear to all the eternal
laws that reign about his house" lives, "motionless as he
is . . . in reality a deeper, more human, and more univer-
sal life than the lover who strangles his mistress, the cap-
tain who conquers in battle, or the husband who avenges
his honor." It was, in short, the Maeterlinck who had
spurned the machine-made patterns of the drama and formulated a new conception of the dramatic to whom Strindberg turned, finding a kinship in his mysticism, admiring
his flights from the factual, his mood-dramas, his unreality.

Just when Europe was witnessing a rebirth of romanticism in the plays of Rostand, D'Annunzio, Benelli,
Stephen Phillips, and Von Hofmannsthal, the beginnings
of the Expressionistic tendency were making themselves
felt. Strindberg, who had been a symbolist in *Lucky Peer*,
was, in *The Dream Play*, *The Spook Sonata*, the two parts
of *The Dance of Life* and the three parts of *Towards
Damascus* blazing new dramatic trails and abandoning
Naturalism. Furthermore—and this was particularly important in the light of what followed—he was turning to
the dream as a theatrical device suited to his new aims. It
was not, of course, the hoary old dream trick which so
many plays had made familiar. No longer did a leading
character, who was sipping a whisky and soda before a
roaring fire in a wainscoted room, doze off, at the end of
the first act, into a sleep which found him a knight at the
Round Table in the second, and awake in the third. The
dream was now to be used not as means for such Con-
necticut Yankee charades, but as a legitimate springboard
to the unedited, uninhibited wanderings of the mind. It
was now to become a psychological instead of a fairy tale
device.

Strindberg and Wedekind, the Wedekind of *Erdgeist*,
Pandora's Box and *The Awakening of Spring*, with his
Earth Spirit, his impatience with an over-literary world,
and his frank delineation of passion and sex, were the
precursors. In Russia Andreyev and Evreinov followed,

Andreyev, with such a symbolic fable of the cycle of existence as *The Life of Man,* or much later, such reachings for philosophical truth as *He Who Gets Slapped* or *The Waltz of the Dogs;* Evreinov with the idea of "Monodrama" and such plays as *The Theatre of the Soul,* or such a masked comedy of appearances and illusion as *The Chief Thing.*

It was in Germany, however, and particularly in the Germany of war and post-war days that Expressionism assumed the staccato scene sequence which is usually associated with its name. The works of Kaiser, Toller and Hasenclever offered new examples of construction, more marked in their tendencies and aggressive in their individuality than the first steps of the forerunners had been, definite enough in fact to warrant the tag which their common characteristics won for them. They came as dramas of disillusionment, of social unrest and tormented mortals. Depending as a rule on only a few indicative properties and cut-outs picked out by sharp shafts of light which stabbed the darkness of stages surrounded by black curtains, their simple production demands were, no doubt, conveniently adapted to the financial capacities of an impoverished Germany. But it must not be supposed that they were only the children of poverty. Instead they were the offspring of human and artistic discontent, born of a rich zest for adventure, children of the spirit and not of the purse. And in such a swift, concentrated biography as Kaiser's *From Morn Till Midnight;* such dramas of rebellion as Toller's *Man and the Masses* and *The Machine Wreckers*—so different as they are from the external approaches to class conflicts of an earlier day like Hauptmann's *The Weavers* or Galsworthy's *Strife;* such a saga of industrialism as Kaiser's *Gas;* or such a tragedy of secret yearnings as Hasenclever's *Beyond,* where a man and a woman speak freely to each other from the hidden language of the mind, the way was pointed to some of the uses to which Expressionism was later to be put.

Post-war France also felt the tidal wave of protest, the

reaction against the old clichés. To a theatre that was as
dead and sterile as that to which Antoine had once brought
the breath of life, came a new generation of playwrights,
men like Pellerin, Gantillon, and Lenormand: Pellerin,
who wrote *Têtes de Rechanges* in which a man leaves for
dinner as one individual only to find on reaching his des-
tination that he has separated into six different and distinct
persons; Gantillon, who in *Maya* found a symbol for illusion in the person of a Marseilles prostitute because she was
a different woman to each man who sought her out, fash-
ioned in the image of his particular need or desire; and
Lenormand who in *The Failures* told with an unswerving
directness the poignant story of the misfortunes which
overtake a tenth-rate actress and her author-husband who
follows her on the road. Such instances picked at random
from a crowded list are typical, nothing more. Nor were
France and Germany the only countries to react to the
new tendencies.

From Czecho-Slovakia came Frantizek Langer with
Peripherie; from Russia Ossip Dymow with *Nju*; from
England has recently come Velona Pilcher with *The
Searcher*. Italy, too, made its contributions in Pirandello
and Rosso de San Secondo who, though they used the traditional forms of the regulation play, belonged by every
philosophical and spiritual right to the new order, and
proved their kinship to it by their endless search for truth
and their continual tracking down of illusion and the mul-
tiplicity of fact and appearance. From Hungary came Mol-
nar's *Liliom*, only another indication of the change, illus-
trating the new viewpoint particularly in its Heaven scene
where Paradise is shown not as a place of pearly gates or
celestial dignity but as a petty police court, because the
dramatist is allowing his audience to see it through the
mind's eye of his principal character, a bum, whose earthly
experiences have given him no other idea of divine justice.

America, too, the America of the skyscraper and the
jazz age, the land of machinery, of standardization and
vaudeville, the saxophone and the Blues, with a thousand

native rhythms and a tempo of life peculiarly suited to such acceleration and distortion, responded to the new impulse. So far the most notable results have been seen in the vivid, simultaneous, omniscient flashes of biography which John Howard Lawson's *Roger Bloomer* revealed, and in the strident, vaudeville insistency of that same Mr. Lawson's *Processional*; in the sordid tragedy of a "Guy" and a "Jane" that Francis Edwards Faragoh set against the pushing, impersonal background of New York in *Pinwheel*; in some of the fine, singing moments of John Dos Passos' *The Moon is a Gong*; in the earlier half of Elmer Rice's stingingly satirical *The Adding Machine*; and in such familiar examples as Eugene O'Neill's *The Emperor Jones* and *The Hairy Ape*.

Regardless of the slim merits of many of the plays built in the image of Expressionism, and even of the faults of monotony and obscurity which often mar the best of them, these dramas come as tokens of revolt. They, too, are attempts to "throw down the old plastering that," as Hugo said, "conceals the façade of art," and must always conceal it for each new generation until it has found a medium of expression true to itself and native to its own time. They are attempts to break from the "well-made play" Scribe established; sallies against the Naturalism for which Antoine fought. They speak from the mind of a new day, using its idiom, catching something of its rhythm, answering some of its needs, and following the pace it sets for them. These authors feel with Velona Pitcher that "a show on the stage should not be an imitation, but an expansion of experience," that "walls should not be built about a vision of life to keep in illusion if they keep out illumination," that "dramatic speech should not be daily dialogue, but something wonderfully different," that "a miracle of mimicry is not worth an ounce of imagination" . . . and, finally, that, "theatre life of the twentieth century cannot . . . be confined behind a conventional fourth wall while the rest of the world is exploring the fourth dimension."

The plays of these dramatists are not only tokens of protest but also symbols of vitality. For they at least show that the modern playwright, who has lagged behind his theatrical co-workers in pliancy and courage, has awakened to experiment and shown a willingness to try and plant his flag on new dominions of his own discovery. And as such they are hopeful symbols, encouraging portents that are not to be despised. Because, in its last analysis, the theatre of each age is forever at the mercy of its playwrights. Only when their courage is high, their imagination unfettered, and the hot blood of protest is running through their veins can its other artists be granted those opportunities which call forth their best talents and give the theatre that quality of being theatre, and being proud of the fact, which is its one condition of glory.

CHAPTER SIX

Russia's Theatre of Social Revolt *

UNIQUE among all recent forms of theatre protest, and different in a thousand basic ways from such revolts in esthetic theory as the Romantics, the Naturalists, the New Movement and the Expressionists represented, is that crudely vital theatre which has invaded and conquered the playhouses of Moscow and Leningrad during the first eleven years of the Soviet Rule in Russia. Here is a very special kind of theatre, the reflection of a very definite kind of social protest, that knows no parallel in the world to-day. It is, of course, the Theatre of the Revolution, belonging to the proletarians, nurtured by the protecults, and indigenous to the emotions and the moment in Moscow. In these respects, as in many others, it is different even among its many distinguished Russian predecessors. The Moscow Art Theatre, in which spiritual realism rose to unequaled heights of perfection; the Musical Studio, with its tingling stylizations of *Lysistrata* and *Carmencita*; the Habima, in which the religious ecstasy of a Hebrew company gave a strange and stirring quality to its performances; and Bailieff, with the rippling gayety of his *Chauve-Souris* that was so reminiscent of the old régime, have crossed the Atlantic and been understood. But the vivid propagandist theatre of the Revolution, unlike the theatre forms which have originated in artistic protest alone, can never survive transplanting. To be understood it must be seen in its native setting. It needs the shadows of the Kremlin and the flaming banners of Moscow's Comintern, or Leningrad's bleeding memories of October, before its voice can roar with the thunder of complete authority.

The productions of the new theatre of Communist

* Reprinted, with alterations, through the courtesy of The Atlantic Monthly.

Russia which are recorded in the State Bakhrushin Theatre Museum and which are actually to be seen in Moscow at Meyerhold's Theatre, the Theatre of the Revolution, the Satiric Theatre, the playhouses in the parks, the working-men's clubs, and which have even forced their way in a modified form to the stages of the Moscow Art Theatre, the Musical Studio, and Tairov's Kamerny Theatre, are phenomena, isolated in aim and method from all other productions the contemporary theatre offers. All of them bear in some degree the stamp of Vsevolod Meyerhold's personality, for he is the "Citizen's Artist" who plays in the revolutionary theatre the role Stanislavsky played in the bourgeois theatre. As a daring and violent innovator, and a tireless agitator, he has led his compatriots in dedicating the revolutionary theatre to the masses in those dirty, milling streets of Red Russia. It is so much a part of them, and they are so much a part of it, that it is almost impossible to tell where the drama of the street leaves off and the drama of the playhouses begins.

It is the drama of the streets, however, and particularly of the streets of Moscow, which is an essential background to the shrill turbulence of the Soviet theatres. It is Moscow, moldering, Asiatic, and mud-splashed, with its glittering star-spangled onion domes, the blues and reds and faded yellow of its old buildings, and the dull gray masses or fresh white horizontal planes of the recent structures of the machine age, that is the scenery which is always present in the minds of the men and women who meet in the playhouses to look at the bare brick walls of the stages which scowl at them from behind the zigzag outlines of Constructivist settings. It is Moscow, awakened from slumbering past, half conscious of an uncomfortable present, and dreamily idealizing a difficult future, that is the heart and head of all that is happening throughout the vast stretches of the U. S. S. R.—a city quivering with a mysterious and exciting vitality that somehow surges upward through all its dreary ugliness—stern, relentless, and triumphant.

For melodramatic contrasts Moscow is without an equal. The most flagrant of these is, of course, the everpresent paradox of a crumbling, malodorous Oriental capital, at least, two hundred years behind the rest of the world when judged by all the usual tokens of enlightenment, boldly striking out to realize a Marxian Utopia by methods no other nation would dare to try even if it wanted to. Other contrasts are to be found at every step—in the Royal Riding School, now used as a public garage; in the famous inscription, "Religion is an opiate for the people," which looks down on the little Iberian chapel ignored by the peasants, who continue to prostrate themselves before its ancient icon; and even in the coronation square of the Kremlin itself, which now resounds to the lusty choruses of passing squads of a Citizens' Army. These are but a few physical symbols, and minor ones at that, of the silent conflict the new Moscow is daily waging with its past. Even a revolution has not been able to readjust the solid stones of architecture to the needs of a new and totally different government. Accordingly, the Revolution seems still to be fought in the streets, waged now with a melancholy irony instead of shrapnel, between the old buildings and the new purposes they serve and the new people they house.

That it is a new people is affirmed by every minute spent in the streets, the stores, the hotels, restaurants, trams, and stations—a new people in command, as new to Moscow as they are to the rest of the world. It is when this drab proletarian army is seen, and then alone, that the propagandist theatre which feeds it becomes explicable. Surely Moscow affords no greater shock to the foreigner than his initial impact with its citizenry. For the first time the wholesale social change, and the sacrifices, following in the wake of the Revolution, of all those minor manifestations of comfort and luxury which we take for granted without ever stopping to consider how much they contribute to the dignity of everyday life, are made brutally clear. These men and women, though assembled from all

corners of the Union, present, when first seen, fewer contrasts than the people of any other metropolis. In fact, in
a city which is alive with every shading of variety, they
alone are robbed of it. The color of individuality seems to
have faded from them. The men, with their gray blouses,
black trousers and boots or burlap shoes, and the women,
with their shawls and shapeless calicoes, fuse into a mighty,
unified host of workers, almost as strictly uniformed as
soldiers, and apparently as forced as they are to submerge
their personalities beneath the clothing that is common to
them all. It is only after several days of being one of them,
when the eye is adjusted and the mind relaxed and the
heart quickened to an imminent sense of something terrible and great in the air, that the foreigner is able to see
the individuals hidden in the mobs.

They are the army of the down-trodden, now in command. To-day Moscow is their city, Russia their country,
and the world their dream. They swarm over the city's
full length, penetrate the chandeliered dining rooms of the
best hotels, sit in the imperial boxes at the theatre, inhabit
the houses of the fallen bourgeoisie, and spend their vaca-
tions in the rest camps made from the estates of the old
nobility. If they are not equally rich, they are all equally
poor. Their sad past has given most of them the patience
and the courage to put up with the discomforts brought
on by the Revolution, and enabled them to consider the
present only an unavoidable period of transition and experiment. More backward than the laborers of any other
country, held down through long centuries of serfdom
and illiteracy, accustomed to few conveniences and no
comforts, these new people have been able to bring but
few of the requisites of living to their new liberty. They
are a simple, grim, robust, and slightly bewildered horde,
whose men are without vanity and whose women are
without coquetry. They crowd the markets, the Soviet
stores, and every inch of ancient Moscow, and their
strong, bronzed peasant bodies gleam naked in the summer's sun on the bathing beaches by the brown water of

the city's canals. The elegancies and refinements which the former ruling classes demanded and enjoyed have slipped into oblivion. With the triumph of this particular proletariat style and beauty in a thousand minor forms, individual taste and all the by-products of sophistication have, temporarily at least, been blotted out.

For the most part, however, these new people seem happy and contented. Having once realized that the Revolution did not mean the end of all work they are slowly waking to the new privileges within their reach. They have gone back to their daily chores with a new sense of the importance of their labors. They haggle in the markets, wait patiently for the clerks in stores and banks alike to do their sums on the wooden balls of Chinese counting boards, and push forward good-naturedly in their crowded but efficient street cars. Their jawbones rotate with an almost American tempo as they chew sunflower seeds and spit out the shells wherever they happen to be. They can be seen clustering in front of the innumerable little booths on the sidewalks, or standing knee-deep in the forest of uncut grass which fringes the streets. Often they bounce over the cobblestones of the tortuous thoroughfares in their springless wagons—dead drunk, with their eyes glazed and their legs seeming to walk on air as they dangle over the sides. The luckier and more impetuous ones loll back on the filthy seats of droshkies that have not been cleaned since the war, their legs sprawled over the potato sacks they are carrying, or their arms clutched tightly around big-horn gramophones of a prehistoric vintage.

What their life lacks in those incidentals that are imperative to our happiness is apparently small cause of complaint to them. In spite of the woeful overcrowding of their living conditions, their poverty, or their dirt, they feel they suffer in a good cause. Because when all is said and done is not Karl Marx in his heaven and all right with the world? And they can seek a welcome forgetfulness in the rationed quota of vodka they are allowed each day. They do not miss what they have never had, nor are they

far enough along in education or prosperity to have been
fully tested by their dearth of comforts. Even their lack
of liberty under the iron dictatorship of the new régime
must seem to the toilers of Moscow an advance on what
is in the background of their experience. It is, at any rate,
a government that proudly proclaims it is of and for the
working classes, and shows its good intentions in a thousand ways. Its rigid supervision, which to the world at
large may seem only another form of Fascist coercion,
cannot surprise a people who have been brought up on the
old secret service, and to whom *lettres de cachet*, mysterious executions, and Siberia have been familiar as far back
as they can remember. This government speaks as the
people's organ, faces cruelly difficult times, and has the
perpetual alibi of continuing what is virtually a period of
martial law until it is strong enough to encourage or
tolerate an opposition.

The real victims of the new régime have, of course, been
wiped out by death or exile or forced into a voiceless retire-
ment. The majority of those who remain and crowd the
streets of Moscow cannot have suffered by the adoption of
Communism. Having for so long been property themselves, they were peculiary susceptible to the idea of eradi-
cating everything for which it stood. Even its perquisites
have come to symbolize for them all the vices of the
bourgeoisie and capitalism. This new citizenry, ignored
and despised by the old government, has suddenly found
itself courted by the new one, and taught to believe, in
theory at least, that it is itself the government. And it is
in that other side of the picture, and the side which deals
not with the people but with what is being done to them,
that the second explanation of the revolutionary theatre
lies.

No authority could have been quicker to utilize every
means at their command to win support and keep their
constituents inflamed than the Soviets. They have watched
and edited the public press with a jealous, all-seeing eye.
They have sent out special exhibition trains to teach the

peasants, opened a Museum of the Revolution in every major city and a Red Corner or a Lenin Room in almost every public building. Under them has been sponsored and organized a network of clubs and unions, which are an informal and invaluable means of instructing the people as well as feeling their pulse. Inspired by what amounts to genius, they have left the worst relics of Tsarism—the ugliest statues and the most hideously furnished palaces—intact as a visual plea against the bad taste of Kings. In many of Moscow's largest squares they have set up radios to bark out the news of the day to illiterates in the voices and phrases of the government. They have suppressed all forms of opposition, and watched the frontiers for dangerous literature which might mislead their people. Nor have they forgotten the youth of the country, because they are wise enough to see that the real test of Sovietism will come with the next generation and prosperity. Accordingly they have organized the children as militantly as Mussolini has in Italy, and taken every precaution to train them in the new order. By fostering a particularly telling form of the poster art, and instigating innumerable pageants to celebrate the triumphs of October, they have, in short, fed the people on all conceivable forms of propaganda ever since the fall of Kerensky's provisional government. It was inevitable that a government which is in advance of every other government in its scientific mastery of the art of propaganda should sooner or later realize the importance of the motion pictures and the stage as instruments of propaganda. That the Soviet Union perceived their extraordinary value from the beginning is both a credit to its perspicacity and an explanation of what the last twelve years have meant to the Russian Theatre.

Faced, first of all, with the tantamount problem of winning the public, then of unifying and controlling it, and finally of keeping it stirred to a constant pitch of dedication and excitement, the government has found the theatre a meeting place ideally suited to its needs. Here was a forum where all the usual rigmarole of a political meeting—the facts, statistics, and appeals to the reason of a backward people—could be dispensed with, a rostrum from which the authorities could reach out with the utmost directness and touch the emotions of their voters.

The government knew, as all theatre people know, that an audience does not meet to exercise its logic, to heckle, or to interrupt. It assembles not to tell but to be told, not to debate but to hear a story. The more unsophisticated it is as an audience, the more it wants its thinking done for it, and the more it craves its villains painted in bold, broad, unmistakable strokes. It is not concerned with whether the cards are stacked or not. In fact, when they are stacked against a common enemy,—whether Punch in the *guignols* of the Parisian boulevards, or the "Huns" in an American war play,—the audience enjoys itself all the more, because it then feels that its secret emotions of cruelty and hatred not only can be released, but are being publicly condoned and justified. If an audience is at all times at the mercy of its theatre, asking only to be amused or moved or interested, it is in any time of public upheaval particularly easy prey. When the bands are playing, the flags waving, and common foes are introduced upon the stage, and playwrights and managers turn the theatres into but ill-disguised recruiting stations, then an audience is receptivity itself.

In Russia there has been, and is, so much drama being acted outside of the playhouses, and drama in which the public plays a prominent and heroic part, that the audience is half conquered from the theatre point of view even before it enters the auditorium. Particularly in Moscow and Leningrad, where the spirit of revolt fermented into decisive action, audiences bring an emotion to the plays they are given which is already strong enough to put flesh and blood upon the skeleton of any drama they may be asked to see. Their theatre is not a world apart, where they can forget themselves. They have not as yet been granted any productions devised purely for the recreation of tired revolutionists. During the eleven years of the Soviet régime they have been asked to remember themselves and hate their enemies, to be aware of this present which is theirs and prepared for the future to which it may lead. Such, in fact, is their momentary fervor that the merest mention of Lenin's name by a captured American soldier in such a play as *The Armored Car* can arouse an audience to a pitch of enthusiasm that a big scene, built up to by a whole act of steady preparation could not equal in the theatre of other countries. Hence it is that the foreigner, unless he has some personal inkling of what these last eleven years have meant to the workers of Russia, and has actually seen them in the grip of their new ideas and fresh surroundings, is often both puzzled and unmoved by what is obviously most affecting in their productions. The emotions of the Soviets are fired not half so much by the technique of their dramatists as by the preparation of their politics. For theirs is a uniquely local and topical theatre, which belongs to and exists for the new people of the new Russia. Without them it would fall on deaf ears, for they are its only consideration. As a result, it is the details of their daily life, the events of proletarian history which they have shaped, the wickedness of those who have oppressed them or who are now opposing them, that are the incessant subjects of their plays.

The Soviet Government, and the more radical theatre agitators, have not stopped here. Nor have their instructions ended with the strains of the *Internationale* or with splashing the old régime with mud. They have had positive theories to spread and new ideals to preach. And these are linked up heart and soul with the focusing of the new order and the character of the new theatre. Holding the individual in but slight esteem, and trying to persuade him that the "mass soul" should be substituted for religions which hope to save the individual soul, the authorities have devoted their stages to spreading the doctrines of the "superpersonal" and the idea of "collective man." Even Meyerhold, the greatest of the modern Russian theatrical insurgents, is quoted by Réné Fülöp-Miller in the *Mind and Face of Bolshevism* as saying that the purpose of the stage is to organize the mass collectively, and that the principles of the propagandist theatre are "in entire conformity with those of Marxism, because they try to emphasize the elements which make prominent what is common to all men, the *unindividual!*" With such an ideal, it is not strange that phrases like "little rickety ego," "worthless soul junk," and "cracking the old nuts of psychological riddles" should be freely used against the realistic theatre to which we, and the world at large, are accustomed. Nor is it odd that, in the place of our dramas which revolve around the particularized love of one Jack for his Jill, and which are acted in one drawing room or kitchen, a new type of play should evolve, set in a new manner.

Certainly it is not odd when the social background of this propagandist theatre is remembered. And it seems almost inescapable when that background is coupled with the managerial problems faced by the insurgent directors. Theirs has been a task which not only involved persuasion, but which also had to find means of persuasion that would appeal to their new public. Their public was, to a large extent, as new to the theatre as it was unaccustomed to holding the reins of power as Stanislavsky has recounted in a fine chapter in *My Life and Art*. Since the Soviet authorities were inciting the people to a deep detestation of everything for which the bourgeoisie had stood, all the bourgeois interiors that had been an integral part of the old realistic theatres were denied them. The old methods could only arouse either a sentimental or a jealous curiosity concerning the comforts of the old régime. Moreover, on those who had not lived in bourgeois interiors, the labor of reproducing them meticulously in the theatre would have been wasted, as their details would have lost their claims to recognition and hence to realism. This new public had the same right that the old public had exercised, of seeing their plays set in a setting which had its roots in their everyday experience.

Accordingly, as a final burning of all bridges that might possibly connect the present with the past, and as a bold glorification of the machines of the industrial age which was at hand, and the so-called Constructivist settings of the revolutionary theatre came into being. They had, as things most generally do have that are the product of necessity, both logic and meaning behind them. The Constructivists waged a rebellious war on beauty, as the Western theatre understands it, and dedicated themselves to the gaunt ribs and bare platforms of functionalism. On their stages, at any rate, as they could not possibly hope to do with the old buildings of Moscow and Leningrad, the Soviets were able to raise structures which caught the spirit of the present and the mood of labor. Instead of aiming to use the stage as a camera by which elaborate interiors could be photographed and "the fourth wall" removed for the delectation of this public that knew nothing about the other three walls, the radical designers sought the laths and beams and whirring wheels of machinery which was the ideal of the new proletarian State. Looking westward to New York, as the supreme achievement of mechanization, they found in the red steel ribs of its unfinished skyscrapers a basis for the physical aspect of their workingmen's theatre. Paint and canvas and all the pretty knicknacks of realism were relegated to the dustbin, and the decorative was left "to the secessionists and the Vienna and Munich restaurants." The cry of the industrial present, which was to prove to the workingman the dignity of being one of many, working at machines for the good of all, was for the sternly practical. The ornamental was despised for its past, and hated as the flowering of a decadent and acquisitive idleness. In its place, the crude, sweaty tools and outlines of the factories were reared upon the propagandist stages, symbolizing the present, and encouraging backward Russia to take its place among the industrial nations of the earth.

With their levels and platforms, elevators and whirling circles within circles, and their vehement avoidance of reality, these new settings—whether they were Constructivist in the most literal meaning of the word, or whether they were influenced only by its spirit—quite naturally revolutionized all the arts of the theatre they served. The old conception of the representational theatre was banished as a relic of the past, or permitted to continue, as in the case of the Moscow Art Theatre, out of reverence and love, in an eddy apart from, and generally untouched by, the mad current of reform. In its place a new ideal was introduced, the ideal of the "theatre theatrical." In their special usage of the phrases Meyerhold and his disciples meant simply a theatre which was proud to confess at all times and in all ways that it was a theatre, which never devoted itself to being a slavish imitation of life, and which withheld no secrets from its audiences. When the Russian radicals broke with realism and put their theories into practice, instead of turning to the wagon, sinking, or revolving stages of the Germans, or any of the other contraptions devised to create illusion, they cleared their stages of machines, because the new Constructivist settings were in themselves machines which had the additional merit of functioning in full view of the spectators. Nor did the revolutionists, when their theatre was performing such a definite social service seek the abstract forms of beauty sought by the Expressionists of post-war Europe and America. Though the new directors shared with the Expressionists the conviction that realism had had its day, they had a different substitute in mind, intended for a different audience. As proletarians these *regisseurs* wanted to share their backstages collectively with proletarian audiences.

Accordingly, Meyerhold and his followers came to regard the front curtain of their theatres as a symbol of the old-fashioned "peep show" theatre, and allowed their audiences to take their seats facing a stage already set in the image of their own factory life. Nor did they allow the curtain to be lowered between the acts, or make any such concessions to a habit of the past that was foreign to their present purpose. If there were changes of scene to make, the directors sent their scene-shifters on in overalls to rearrange the setting and show that workingmen were assisting in the performance. And, as directors of a propagandist theatre that worshiped all that was practical, they left the brick walls of the back stage bare and undecorated behind their settings as a final tribute to functionalism. Believing as they did, and do, in the glorification of the practical, they were proud to grant the naked bricks of the back stage a dignity which the realistic theatre had consistently denied them.

On such a stage and in such a theatre, it was inevitable that the actor should have to make violent readjustments. Certainly a theatre dedicated to the "unindividual" must have cost the old-time performers untold difficulties, to say nothing of humiliations. In the theatre the world over, the actor, whether he is encouraged to believe it or not, considers his task the supreme expression of his individuality. His justification is a more than logical one, because he, of all artists, has only himself and his own body to use as a medium of expression. In the Soviet theatre he was asked to forget almost everything he knew and lived by and try to become merely a member of the masses, acting very often in overalls. His ears, not to mention his pride, must have been considerably stunned by such a phrase as that of Meyerhold's in which the actor was told that he was no longer a star, acting for his own aggrandizement, but "an instrument for social manifestoes." Furthermore, he was informed that to survive he must feel himself a vital part of the new society and the new stage. If he was accustomed to the easy-chairs and ash trays of the old methods, Constructivism must have come as an unwelcome innovation. Its perilous levels not only violated all the old rules of "center stage," and controlling a scene, but demanded an entirely new style of acting. Often he was told that to catch the new rhythms he must forget himself and become an acrobat among acrobats. He, too, must serve the machines and perfect himself in the dynamic movements that are known in Russia as "bio-mechanics." The cultivation of his body was what he owed to society, and the subjugation of his individuality was what he owed to the stage. He could no longer indulge even in the pleasant details of veraciously observed character acting, in which Russian actors had always excelled with particular distinction. For the dizzy structure behind him, he must find a new, broad, unreal, exaggerated, posteresque enlargement adapted to it. He must excel at "grotesques," caricature, horseplay, and violent, stirring movement, and, as a member of the masses, devote himself to serving them.

As a theatre without contemporary precedent, its form has been restricted by none of those inhibitions which are commonly known as conventions. Its playwrights, as well as its directors, have felt free in blazing a trail, to choose any materials or combinations of material so long as they have their proper effect upon a proletarian audience. The playwrights, like the actors, found their profession reoriented. Everything they remembered in the dramatic practice of their own or other literature they were asked to forget. Speaking to a new audience, they had to aim at an untried and different denominator of the intellect as well as of the emotion. Their chambermaids and butlers and all the worn devices they had relied on to oil the genteel drama of the past, were prescribed. In a world where every one was of one class, where titles were done away with and officials hailed waiters as comrades, there was no longer any justification for presenting menials on the stage who had nothing better to do than to talk conveniently about their master's business.

That favorite pastime of "bourgeois" playwrights of using a microscope to study the sufferings of small and great souls, was also listed as the supercargo of the past. "Soul junk" and "rickety ego" hurt the dramatists' inherited subject matter as much as it wounded the actor's pride, because with the glorification of the "unindividual,"

the playwrights were suddenly forced to forget particularized characters for bluntly outlined types. All their
painfully learned tricks of creating illusion, their "cover
scenes," delayed climaxes, and the rest, were swept aside
with one decisive gesture by the lightning tempo and
physical differences of the new methods. What must have
been most difficult of all, however, was that these propagandist playwrights found they could no longer flirt with
the theories of futility which had been the mainstay of
Russian dramatists for several generations. In the place of
the "Russian soul," the unhappy Annas and Fedyas whose
despairing inertia had sent them slowly to a suicide's grave,
they were asked to put the "mass soul" of victorious
workers and sing the joys of collective man. Their audiences were not any more concerned with refinements inside the theatre than outside, and did not want their
problems or their emotions obscured by any of the am-
bushes so sacred to gentility. They wanted them raw and
tingling, outspoken and obvious.

Outside of the playhouses, the workingman found that
his old religion and all of its glamorous superstitions were
being discouraged. He was being told that the faith in
which he had been reared was his enemy, an opiate
for his mind and a foe to the government of which he
was a part. He had even seen several of his most holy
cathedrals closed as houses of God and reopened as people's
museums. He could observe, too, in the hundreds of
churches the government did not close, the empty frames
from which sacred icons that contained stones or metals
of any value had been taken by the authorities as a means
of saving Soviet Russia in the darkest hours of her public
credit. Though he knew his government stood in theory
for religious toleration, he was given to understand that
an age of reason was at hand. He was encouraged—as an
act of reason—to worship the machines, which would bring
him immediate well-being, rather than the holy images,
which could offer him no practical benefits. But whether
the churches or the machines were to be an outlet of his

ecstasy and superstition had but little to do with the fact
that he was both superstitious and ecstatic by temperament.
No legislative act could rob him of that part of his being
he had known as his "soul." No one was more aware of this
than the authorities, or more aware that a people trained to
being onlookers at processions of a visual splendor the
modern world has rarely equaled could not suddenly be
deprived of their ceremonies and their ritual and remain
contented. With uncanny wisdom, the authorities did not
try to change the spirit of the worker's heart, but to
divert it into a new outlet. They opened the doors to the
playhouses at the lowest possible cost a generous official
subsidy would permit, and allowed the workingman to
carry into the theatre something of the fervor he had
brought to his churches. They designed the new productions to satisfy this among other needs, and in Karl Marx
and Lenin they provided him with the real gods of the
moment of emancipation, even though by doing so they
seemed to contradict their theory of the "unindividual."
In short, in an age turbulently alive to the excitements
of liberty, they gave the people a theatre which was, in its
last analysis, only a High Mass sung to the spirit of revolution.

To satisfy this new need, the playwrights sought constantly to keep the fervor of victory alive and achieve an
ecstasy worthy of a paradise that was being realized for
the first time. They forgot style and all the usual embel-
lishments of language and took the heart of the common
people as their target. In words as simple and unorna-
mented as Lenin's own, they reached out for the new public before them, employing catchwords of the moment to
excellent advantage, and drumming in their points by effective repetition. The themes of their plays became jour-
nalistic and topical. They wrote government editorials in
the form of headlines and told them with the relentless
visualization of the tabloids. Where they were afraid a
point might pass unnoticed, they set up a silver screen
above their stages and ran ringing shibboleths upon it to

accompany the action. The present was, quite naturally, their province, the present of the proletariat, as *The Wheels Are Turning, Mandate, Soufflé,* and any number of their dramas prove. They were, however, allowed to make excursions into the past, but they looked backward only to fortify and justify the present. If they revived a classic, such as in *The Inspector General,* or *Intelligence Comes to Grief,* in their most revolutionary theatres, they felt at liberty to alter its text and meaning to suit their aims. To them history was, and is, a mine rich in the ores of Tsarist villainies or glorious with the misfortunes of early revolutionists, as is indicated by *1881, The Decembrists,* and *The Plot of the Empress* (the last Tsarina, of course, and Rasputin).

When not concerned with history, or Soviet uprisings, or the wonders of Communism, or the need of the sports, the playwrights have been permitted to graze elsewhere to find illustrations of the downtrodden whom Soviet Russia may save. American and English capitalists were villains ready-made to fit their needs, and they were introduced upon the stage as drooling fools whose hearts were as black as the records of their past, as *D. E. (The Destruction of Europe)* and *Roar China* testify. Even in the old Imperial Opera House in Moscow, now owned and operated by the State, the voice of the Soviet raises itself above the clamor of the orchestra, and a new opera, like *The Red Poppy,* shows a Russian crew come to the defense of some oppressed coolies and ends with the waving of the red flag. And often, too, when the playwrights invite the proletarians to wander from their local problems, they show them the proletarians of other countries shaking off the shackles of capitalistic bondage. The hope of a world uprising of the masses is kept steadily before them, because the radical directors have realized with Lenin that "one must have something to dream of."

Outside of the regular propagandist theatres, such as Meyerhold's or the Theatre of the Revolution, the work of flag waving and propagandizing goes on with the same insistency. Though Tairov and Stanislavsky may hold back from its most violent forms of expression, its methods spill over into a thousand different outlets. Especially in the workingmen's clubs and unions, which operate even in farthest Siberia, the theatre is the servant of the new State. In the Blue Blouse performances of the clubs it takes the pleasant form of amateur vaudeville, and includes sports numbers, timely songs, playlets, humorous speeches, and unavoidable jingles at the expense of Chamberlain—who, by the way, is not only a favorite joke of the Russians, but is also the symbol of European capitalism, shot in the shooting galleries and burned in effigy in the streets. Or propaganda lifts its head in the thin disguise of *Living Newspapers,* those pointed charades that the government has found so effective in relaying to illiterate groups its own version of the day's news.

It is slight wonder, therefore, that this propagandist theatre should be linked inseparably with the present in Russia, and particularly with all that Moscow stands for as its capital. By its own intention it is not an artist's theatre, and admits no art that exists by and of itself. Its directors have willfully snatched the theatre out of the hazy limbo of the impractical and the purely enter- taining, and forced it into the harshness of public service. They have made a "house organ" of it, and as such it can no more mistake a serious claim of being art, in our sense of the word or in its usual esthetic implication, than can a government pamphlet on horse breeding. It is to the theatre as we understand it, what a Chautauqua is to Shakespeare, what sky writing is to poetry, or what a poster is to a painting. Like the poster, it does not pretend that its beauty is its reason for being. Speaking to the ma- jority, it proscribes all the subtleties that might appeal to the minority. Accordingly it puts a ban on genius and a premium on ingenuity. It is the paradise of the opportu- nist, of the man who is one step ahead of the streets to-day and two steps behind the theatre of next month. It has no time to think of posterity, and hardly enough time to keep up with the present. It is the loud speaker of the masses, and is therefore bound to be more conscious of its public than any New York manager has ever been of his box office. It produces what the government wants the people to want in such a way that they are forced to want it.

Crude, infantile, noisy, obstreperous, cheap, confused, and formless as it is, it has, however, a thrilling quality of life that has made it magnificently successful in being what it set out to be—a propagandist theatre. Already rumors are abroad in Moscow that the proletarians are weary of propaganda and tired of having to consider the waving of a red flag the highest emotional climax a drama can reach. The fact that they were not tired of its shouting and any number of its rasping puerilities nine years ago shows how shrewd this propagandist theatre has been in its attack, and how much it was needed both by the government and by the people. It indicates, too, how skilful the radical producers have been in changing their needles each time so as not to wear out the same old record they have been forced to play over and over again.

Even to its leaders, however, this theatre has not seemed a final form. They know just how precariously topical it is, and how close it is to the need that has mothered it. But to them, imbued as they are with strident and irrepressible social theories, this new theatre does not seem the prostitution of an art that it does to us. They are proud of their success in prostituting an art which they have made their own. Certainly when one measures them by their intentions, or judges them by some of their liberating experiments in technique they have stumbled on to, one must admit that they have reason to be proud. Because both as a herald as an echo to the sufferings and hopes of a sorely tried and yet ecstatic Russia, this propagandist theatre has performed a superb function as the first step toward the true people's theatre which will some day take its place.

SELECTED BIBLIOGRAPHY

In making these brief summaries of a few of those revolts which have charted the course of the modern theatre, the following books and publications have proven themselves of invaluable assistance.

1. THE COMING OF NATURALISM: *Main Currents in Nineteenth Century Literature,* by George Brandes (Boni and Liveright); *European Theories of the Drama,* edited by Barrett H. Clark (Appleton); *Antoine and the Théâtre Libre,* by Samuel Montefiore Waxman (Harvard University Press); "Recollections of the Théâtre Libre," by Andre Antoine (*Theatre Arts Monthly,* March, 1925); *French Dramatists,* by Brander Matthews (Scribners).

2. FREE THEATRES AND NEW PLAYWRIGHTS: "Recollections of the Théâtre Libre, by Andre Antoine (*Theatre Arts Monthly,* March, 1925); *Antoine and the Théâtre Libre,* by S. M. Waxman (Harvard University Press); *An Outline of Contemporary Drama,* by Thomas H. Dickinson (Houghton Mifflin); "Little Theatre Backgrounds," by Kenneth Macgowan in *Theatre,* edited by Edith J. R. Isaacs (Little, Brown); *The Quintessence of Ibsenism,* by George Bernard Shaw (Brentano); *Letters of an Old Playgoer,* edited by Brander Matthews (Dramatic Museum of Columbia); *The Development of Dramatic Art,* by Donald Clive Stuart; *The Path of the Modern Russian Stage,* by Alexander Bakshy (Cecil Palmer and Hayward); *My Life in Art,* by Constantin Stanislavsky (Little, Brown); *Our Irish Theatre,* by Lady Gregory (Putnam's); *Iconoclasts,* by James Huneker

(Scribners); *The Modern Drama*, by Ludwig Lewisohn (Viking Press); *The Contemporary Drama of Italy*, by Lander MacClintock (Little, Brown); *The American Dramatist*, by Montrose J. Moses (Little, Brown); *The Contemporary Drama in Ireland*, by Ernest Boyd (Little, Brown); *The Changing Drama*, by Archibald Henderson (Henry Holt); *Modern Drama in Europe*, by Storm Jameson (Collins); *A Study of Modern Drama*, by Barrett H. Clark (Appleton); *Contemporary French Dramatists*, by Barrett H. Clark (Appleton).

3. THE FOURTH WALL: "Shakespeare the Designer's Touchstone," by John Mason Brown in *Theatre*, edited by Edith J. R. Isaacs (Little, Brown); "What the Moderns Have Done to Shakespeare" (special issue, *Theatre Arts Monthly*, July, 1927); *Shakespeare from Betterton to Irving*, by George C. D. Odell (Scribners); *The Development of Dramatic Art*, by Donald Clive Stuart (Appleton); *An Outline of Contemporary Drama*, by Thomas H. Dickinson (Houghton Mifflin); *Antoine and the Théâtre Libre*, by S. M. Waxman (Harvard University Press); *My Life in Art*, by Constantin Stanislavsky (Little, Brown); *The Theatre Through the Stage Door*, by David Belasco (Harpers).

4. THE VISUAL IMPETUS: *Modern Drama in Europe*, by Storm Jameson (Harcourt, Brace); *The Theatre of Tomorrow*, by Kenneth Macgowan (Boni and Liveright); *Continental Stagecraft*, by Kenneth Macgowan and Robert Edmond Jones (Harcourt Brace); *The New Spirit in Drama and Art*, by Huntly Carter (Mitchell Kennerley); *The New Spirit in the European Theatre, 1914–1924*, by Huntly Carter (Doran); *The Art Theatre*, by Sheldon Cheney (Knopf); *The New Movement in the Theatre*, by Sheldon Cheney (Mitchell Kennerley); *Modern Stage Decoration*, by Sheldon Cheney (John Day); *Twentieth Century Stage Design*, by Sam Hume and Walter Réné Fuerst (Alfred A. Knopf); *Theatre: Essays on the Arts of the Theatre*, edited by Edith J. R. Isaacs; *The Theatre of Today*, by Hiram Kelly Moderwell, new edition, 1927 (Dodd, Mead); *The Flower in Drama, Glamour*, and *Theatre Practice*, by Stark Young (Scribners); *Toward a New Theatre*, by Edward Gordon Craig (Dutton); *Scene*, by Edward Gordon Craig (Oxford University Press); *Modern Theatres*, by Irving Pichel (Harcourt, Brace); *Drawings for the Theatre*, by Robert Edmond Jones (Theatre Arts); *Project for the Theatrical Presentation of Dante's Divine Comedy*, by Norman-Bel Geddes (Theatre Arts); *The Theatre*

of Max Reinhardt, by Huntly Carter (Mitchell Kennerley); *Max Reinhardt and His Theatre*, edited by Oliver M. Sayler (Brentano); *Drama*, by Ashley Dukes (Henry Holt); *Theatre Arts Monthly* and *The Mask*, back files and current issues.

5. PLAYWRIGHTS OF PROTEST: *The Youngest Drama*, by Ashley Dukes (Sergel); *The Drama of Transition*, by Isaac Goldberg (Appleton); *The American Dramatist*, by Montrose J. Moses (Little, Brown); "New Forms for Old," by Rosamond Gilder in *Theatre*, edited by Edith J. R. Isaacs (Little, Brown); *Outline of Contemporary Drama*, by Thomas H. Dickinson (Houghton Mifflin); *The Development of Dramatic Art*, by Donald Clive Stuart (Appleton).

6. RUSSIA'S THEATRE OF SOCIAL REVOLT: *My Life in Art*, by Constantin Stanislavsky (Little, Brown); *The Path of the Modern Russian*, by Alexander Bakshy (Cecil Palmer and Hayward); *The New Theatre and Cinema of Russia*, by Huntly Carter (Chapman and Dodd); *Shifting Scenes*, by Hallie Flanagan (Coward McCann); *The Russian Theatre*, by Oliver M. Sayler (Brentano); *The Mind and Face of Bolshevism*, by Rene Fülöp-Miller (Knopf).

THE END